Also by $\mathcal{R}$*ACHEL* $\mathcal{P}$*EDEN*

RURAL FREE (1961)
THE LAND, THE PEOPLE (1966)

THESE ARE BORZOI BOOKS
published in New York by
ALFRED A. KNOPF, INC.

Speak to the Earth

*S*PEAK
T*O* T*HE* *E*ARTH

Pages from a farmwife's journal

❧ ❧ ❧

By

RACHEL PEDEN

❧

Drawings by *S*IDONIE *C*ORYN

ALFRED A. KNOPF · NEW YORK · 1974

THIS IS A BORZOI BOOK
PUBLISHED BY ALFRED A. KNOPF, INC.

Library of Congress Cataloging in Publication Data

Peden, Rachel.   Speak to the earth.

1. Farm life—Indiana. 2. Nature. I. Title.
S521.5.I6P4   917.72   74–7736
ISBN 0–394–49432–6

Manufactured in the United States of America
First Edition

To GENE C. PULLIAM,
perceptive and sensitive friend,
from whom I learned
you can walk on water
if the right person reaches out
a hand to you

Contents

Acknowledgments

✲ THIS BOOK, like *Rural Free,* and *The Land, The People,* is largely made up of my farm column material that has appeared in the Indianapolis *Star* and the Muncie *Evening Press.* The publisher of these newspapers has wholeheartedly given me permission to use the material, and I am grateful.

I am grateful also to all the people who have let me quote them or write about them or even mention them;

ix

A CKNOWLEDGMENTS

and to Kate Hargrave Smith who first brought the farm column to the attention of the Knopf editor;

and to the copy editor there, whose acute understanding of punctuation, spelling, and English usage enabled him to give the manuscript a kind grooming for the printer.

I am grateful to everyone who had anything to do with this book, including those who waited, and everyone who will ever read it.

As my farmer-husband says in moments of overwhelming gratitude, "Thank you, OH, thank you!"

SPEAK TO THE EARTH

And Also Listen

THE FEBRUARY DAY was ending in a cold sunset; no red clouds, no pinkness, no orange-colored glory. Only a dazzling silver disk in a gray muslin sky; a hill from which bushy, dark trees pushed upward; a wind blowing coldly out of the north.

But the day's meager thawing had sharpened the icicles that hung in a harpstring row from the henhouse

3

roof, and when I brushed my hand across them they fell with a musical shattering.

Passing the big pond back of the barn on my way to the hilltop woods, I noticed four of the farm-hatched, tame mallards had decided to spend the night there, rather than come down to the duck's house and accept confinement with their corn.

The brown water hissed and talked to itself at the pond's rim and I went on. A dog barked, a jet plane passed overhead, invisible in its own thunder. From the woods a bird sang insistently, the same four notes, F♯, E, F♯, D, over and over into a little melody.

Leaves blown along the path behind me sounded like footsteps following. When I reached the hilltop and stopped to look back down at the farmhouse snuggled into its many maples like a cold chin into a fur coat, I shivered and buttoned my jacket collar.

Near last summer's blackberry patch a wild-grape vine lay in a brown heap on the ground, like a raveled hay rope. Slightly beyond the white beehives at the edge of the woods was a young honey locust, gray and entirely dead except for half a dozen savage, bright brown thorns. I thought of Easter.

The woods are fenced with barbed wire to keep out livestock. Following the fenceline on toward the hayfield, I came to the corner post, an old sawed-stone monolith more than five feet high and twenty inches square that originally supported a gate in Benny Whisenand's fence. Gate, fence, and Benny are long since gone, but the rusty iron bolts that supported the gate hinges are still there in the limestone, and every winter late rains brighten the lichened stone from gray to vivid green.

In the field now autumn's late growth of orchard

grass, brown and dead, had collapsed onto its own springy, thick crowns, thus protecting the roots through winter. I fight orchard grass in the garden, where it bulges up like a pillow and resists my hoe, but in the pasture, where as Dick says it is "the first green bite in spring, the last one in the fall," it is valuable both for forage and for soil protection. All winter it had protected the sloping hayfield (Hagerstown silt loam and highly erodable) against cascades of rain and snow. A late-sprouted candle mullein had also taken advantage of the protection and now lay flattened against the field like a green felt rose on a woman's hat.

A farm is a place of opportunity simultaneous with obligation, an immaculate fitting-together of plant and animal life, as well as a place where they compete relentlessly. In the fencerow a young multiflora rose was growing, sprouted no doubt from a seed dropped there from some passing bird that had previously fed on multiflora elsewhere. Symbiotically, the young rosebush had offered its thorny density as anchorage for another bird's nest. Now the empty nest, gray and torn and hanging by a mere fragment of rim, was lifted and dropped by the persistent wind.

This pasture is fertile now and well sodded, but when we came to the farm it was starved and gullied. I remember that sloping field in many different times, all pleasant, for we have lived here a long time now; a son and daughter have grown up and left. And in that time, often, I have remembered the words of Job: "Speak to the earth and it will teach you." It has taught me a great deal, has given me more questions than answers, and I have learned to listen as well as to speak to it.

From the edge of these woods I have dug up pennyroyal and planted it nearer the house. Many afternoons we brought the two children and Rose, the farm Collie, in the wagon to work in this field. Sometimes we brought along a candy bar, and when Rose heard the unwrapping of it, she came expectantly for her share.

In our first years we shucked corn by hand out of that field, and never got done before cold weather. Our son Joe was a little boy then and rode in the wagon while we walked, throwing the corn in around him. When he complained that his feet were cold we stopped and built a little cornstalk fire and the horses rested. It was pleasant. Always, by the time the wagon was filled, the boy was asleep and as we came down the hill the cattle knew the sound and came to meet us. They opened their huge Wyandotte caves of mouth and their long, rough tongues pulled out ears of corn from around the sleeping boy.

One spring afternoon when the mud was a nice workable texture at the edge of the field and Carol was seven, she went on the tractor with Dick to the field, and while he worked, she made a little set of mud dishes for me. Little mud cups and saucers, cream pitcher and sugar bowl, little plates with my initials applied in long, thin rolls of mud. I still have them.

Remembering these things on that cold February evening I looked around the half-circle enclosing the farm and thought how greatly farming has changed since we came here.

In the stillness I could hear even the faint rustle of old grass blades and the rattling of restless, thin leaves on a young beech tree. To what purpose did they cling all winter? Did the tree need them, that they did not fall onto the ground and merge with other leaves into a new usefulness as topsoil? In nature's thrifty routine, nothing is really wasted. The end of one process is the foundation for another, and evolution goes ceaselessly on. It has been millions of years since the thin beginnings of soil were formed by the death of lichens, small plants, then larger ones mingling with acids and rocks and rain.

In the velvety quietness of that February evening the sense of immortality and creation was as distinct as the outline of dark, bare trees in the distant landscape. In the natural world, even in this bleak, least favorite month there is always some commonplace thing offering its portion of truth and beauty. Beauty of stillness, beauty of motion as earth goes about its routine chores.

High above the woods a hawk was flying, as smoothly as water flowing, and with infinite grace. I watched until he was beyond sight, then I turned back toward the house. Across the road, in a neighbor's field, cattle were walking slowly in the brown, wintry cornfield. It was a timeless scene; familiar; commonplace. And beautiful as ancient sorrow.

꒰ AFTER WE BOUGHT Ira and Monta Stanger's farm, which touches this one on the east, with the Maple Grove road running between two fields, we continued to refer to it as "Iry's farm" and "Montie's house." Ira had lived in that house all his sixty-five years. He had inherited the farm from his father, Bent, who had inherited it as his half of his mother's farm. Montie, in her neighborly way, was glad when we bought it. "It'll be kinda like keeping it in the family," she said, and they moved closer to their married daughter.

We were glad to have the one hundred and nine acres to add to our one hundred and thirty, but I missed Montie as a neighbor. She was always generous and warm-hearted, and knew community history and folklore. She was a valuable research source for a person writing a farm column for city newspapers, as I was doing.

Montie always raised a big garden, strawberries, and chickens. She sold dressed chickens and eggs, and Ira worked as a carpenter in town to supplement the farm income. The house always seemed clean and hospitable and it was not until it belonged to us that I discovered its many difficulties.

"I'm going to leave the house clean for you," Montie told me, and did, even to washing and putting back the polka-dotted pink-and-white kitchen curtains. The kitchen walls were pink. Montie liked color and gaiety and live-liness. She liked having colored gloves to match her different dresses, or painting a bright flower border around the living-room door. She never protested when Ira came into the house with his muddy boots on. "It's his house, too," she said. On the other hand, if he came home from a day's work in town and discovered she had made plans to go out that evening, he never protested.

From Montie, I learned farm customs and superstitions and important things like what else you can use for wild greens besides mustard and wild lettuce and lamb's-quarters; you can even use a few tender blackberry leaves.

I was surprised when we were visiting them in their new home one evening and she asked me about feather beds. She held out what looked like a little twirl of feathers, fastened together into a mound about the thickness of two round lunch crackers. "You know," she said, "I bought an old feather bed at Archie Ellett's sale and I've been making pillows out of it. I've made nine big ones and still have enough feathers for anyway three or

8

four more. And this was in it. Every feather bed I've ever ripped up had a little thing like this in it. What does it mean?"

Considering how much beating and fluffing up a feather bed gets, it was surprising that the little mound still held firmly together.

"Sometimes," Montie said, "it was a long strip of cloth with feathers sewed onto it. It must have some meaning. I could have asked Mom, but I just never thought to . . ."

Nobody makes feather beds any more, but they were a standard homemade mattress in early farm homes. Women who kept geese plucked the down from them. When they dressed chickens they saved the small, soft feathers and finally filled a big canvas casing with them. A sleeper's body sank down into deep, soft hollows and every morning the feather bed had to be vigorously shaken to restore its smooth flatness.

I promised to ask about the feather cluster in my column, and when I did, a reader from Greencastle wrote, "They used to tell me that when somebody died on the bed, it was ripped open and searched for the little cluster of feathers. If it was there it meant the person had gone to heaven. There was a name for it, but I forget what it was."

The custom of putting a cluster in the mattress, to make sure the bereaved family would find the comforting hope, was inevitable. Perhaps people didn't really believe it, but just didn't want to overlook any possible comfort. Having learned the legend, if I were making a feather bed I would certainly put in a firmly stitched swirl of feathers.

In its way, a superstition is an expression of faith,

and more than likely in the distant future some of our current, most devout beliefs will have degenerated into mere superstitions.

People used to ridicule the belief that plants do better if the gardener talks to them and shows them affection, but now scientific experiments have provided support for this charming superstition. People used to ridicule the belief that household utensils and farming tools had their individual hostilities or amiabilities. Now science supports this belief by saying all atoms have two tendencies, contradictory, the tendency to cling to and the tendency to fly apart from. This lends validity to the belief that nothing is really inanimate; a cooking pan can be, inherently, as uncooperative as a balking horse or kicking cow.

Some superstitions may have originated from pure coincidence. The belief that if you kill a cricket there will soon be a death in your family, for instance. I don't believe this, but when a cricket gets into the farmhouse, as dozens do in the fall, I never kill it. (Nor bees nor beetles either.) I set a glass over it, slide a stiff paper under it, and carry it outdoors to release it alive. I do this because I believe that in his way the cricket is important to the world, and the world belongs to both of us although in my own house I am in my own territorial imperative and I'd like for him to stay in his. But even in my imperative, where the cricket is disturbing and unwelcome, I realize human welfare depends on nature's keeping the balance which man, in his arrogance and destructive power, continues to upset.

Folklore is usually better supported by evidence than superstition is. Much of it is poetic in expression, and some of it is practical.

"Straight up on end is the wet moon," a farmer said.

"When she's settin' exactly level like a saucer the water can't git out, but when she turns and is standin' straight up on end the water'll run out. We git our rains then, after a long dry spell." There is some scientific basis for Mrs. Jordan's comment: "Rain on the second of June will cut down the blackberry crop." If rain keeps bees away, or washes off the pollen, the bloom may not be properly pollinated, and this will shorten the crop.

Lewis Schafer, thrifty German farmer who never spoke a word of English until he started to a country school and now can't remember any German, advised us to "cut clover on the second Monday in June. Put moth balls in the sweet corn rows to keep coons out of it."

My first Maple Grove neighbor, Rennie Dutton, who taught me how to make lye soap the year wild dogs got into our sheep, and also taught me about making apple butter in a big kettle in her back yard, also told me: "Never make sauerkraut in the sign of the lady with the flower in her hand." (Virgo, the virgin.) "It'll turn soft every time."

In the days when farmers slept on straw mattresses and fleas from the hogs got onto farmers and thence into mattresses, it was thought that pennyroyal would get rid of the fleas in the beds.

A farm apprehension that has almost the status of superstition is the belief that if somebody makes a farmer a reasonable, bona fide offer for a cow, and the farmer doesn't take it, misfortune will overtake her. She may die or fall into a sinkhole or get caught in the fence, or never be able to get in calf.

But it was good, sound understanding of his soil that prompted Old Tom Owens to tell his young share-renters Clint and Bent Stanger: "It's too early to plow."

They protested that other farmers in the community were plowing and Old Tom exploded into a proverb: "One fool makes forty more!"

⬎ AT BREAKFAST, spreading red-raspberry jelly on toast, Dick said, "Carr told me a new cure for lockjaw somebody'd told him the other day."

Neither farmer has ever had lockjaw, but farmers like to know about home cures, just in case. In everyday life a farmer is subject to small injuries from jagged metal, rusty nails, and machinery in which tetanus germs may be lurking. Probably all farmers should have tetanus shots, routinely, just as they vaccinate their hogs against cholera, cattle against blackleg or Bang's disease, and the farm dog against rabies. In Indiana farming is rated the second most hazardous of occupations. Mining is first.

"And Dean Gonce has a remedy for pinworms in children," Dick went on, by this time putting sliced peaches over ice cream. Fortunately a person can go right on drinking black coffee no matter what repulsive thing turns up in the conversation. "You take your penknife and go out and rip the bark off of a peach tree and then shave the inner side of the bark and make a tea of it. Give not more than a teaspoonful for pinworms in children."

I said, "I didn't know Dean had any children."

"Oh, he doesn't. But he gave this tea to a child he saw in Kentucky when he was down there with a load of to-bacco last summer. She was so ill her lips had drawn back and she wasn't eating anything. The next day she ate and drank a little, Dean said."

Dean is a blacksmith. For at least twenty-two years he had a little shop in the run-down part of town that was called Pigeon Hill, and eventually was taken over forcibly in the name of Urban Renewal. Dean drove a hundred miles a day to work the two p.m. through midnight shift at the International Harvester in Indianapolis. When he got home from this job, around two in the morning, he slept a few hours, then worked in his blacksmith shop until noon, when it was time to start back to the city job.

When Urban Renewal started its fight to take over Pigeon Hill, Dean was the last to give in. Finally he bought a small farm west of the old South Union church. There was a little house on it, into which he moved with his wife Ruth. He built a blacksmith shop and a few years later retired from the city job and bought a few beef cattle, for a sideline. He likes that.

"He's old-fashioned about it, though," Dick said. "He says, 'You can't make any money feedin' 'em out of a sack.' He thinks it's enough to give them corn, clover hay, and salt, and maybe a little molasses. He's for fertilizing the fields with manure; uses a little commercial, but not much. Up here on this west pasture I can show you to the very inch where I stopped spreading fertilizer. The cattle eat right to the line and stop."

↘ ALMOST ANY FARMER, about to have a well drilled, calls in a "water witch" to locate the vein. No Indiana farmer calls a water witch a "dowser" or "diviner."

My neighbor Wolcott Telfer, Smith College graduate, Phi Beta Kappa, with a mind omnivorous as a roll-top desk, is not really superstitious, but she has lived in this community several years and respects farm traditions. When the Telfers, prodded by Bob's restlessness, sold their elegant brick house and turned the farm into a housing development, they built themselves a new brick mansion higher up on the hill. Unable to persuade the nearby city to bring water lines into the new development, Wolcott asked Dick, "Who in Maple Grove is a water witch?"

"Fred Henry Dutton," he told her promptly. Fred Henry's grandfather, Emerson Dutton, was a renowned witch. He could even tell the prospective well driller how many feet it was to the water—one foot for every time the forked stick dipped while he held it. People who watched Emerson do this were never surprised when the subsequent digging proved him accurate.

Fred Henry is almost as good at it as Emerson was. Big and easygoing, he loves to sing, fish, and laugh. He lives in a small town and drives a big dairy truck. His wife plays the pipe organ in church and all three of their children have good singing voices.

He cut a forked stick from a peach tree in his own yard and brought it with him to the Telfer house. The new mansion, high up on a hilltop, has a magnificent view that will be ruined when the rest of the farm goes into houses and condominiums. It is enclosed by a long brick wall that follows the incline of the hill down and down, leveling off every now and then into a step, thus making a fine, adventurous walking place for the visiting grandchildren.

Fred Henry stopped here on his way home. "Yeah," he said, "I found a vein near the house. They'll have to go pretty far for water, though. There was a man there diggin' a well for another house. He'd already gone down a hundred and ten feet and hadn't struck water yet. But he will, maybe has by now. I'll go by there sometime and see."

He wouldn't take any money for witching the well, said it would "ruin his professional standing." No cigars, either; he'd given up smoking. A good drink from the well maybe, some thirsty day when he was passing.

❧ IT WAS EVENING. In Claude Martindale's dusty, inviting woodworking shop a tall wood-burning stove gave out a cozy warmth. Piles of wood shavings and some sawdust added a pleasant fragrance.

"We both love to burn wood and I've always wished we had a fireplace in the house," said Mrs. Martindale.

The shop is only a few steps across the yard from the farmhouse kitchen. In its woodsy setting, the Martindale farm has the aura of security and affection a farm takes on when it has belonged to the same family many years. In the long run the land shapes the people, but when one man has owned and worked on one farm a long time it expresses him just as the wrinkles of his coat sleeves express his elbows.

"Lots of people think it's bad luck to burn sassafras," Claude said. His voice is habitually gentle. His eyes are deep brown and kind, with a brightness that suggests he has thought of something to smile about. He has known deep grief, too. When he was a boy eight years old he had an old dog he told his troubles to and, he says, the dog always listened.

He is a deeply religious man. His shop walls are decorated with religious mottoes and a calendar illustrated with a Bible scene. He has been an Elder in the Ellettsville Baptist church longer than any other Elder has served, and he keeps the old church records. When I wanted to write a newspaper column about the church's history, mentioning the time a whole Negro family was received into membership long before integration became a national fever, and the times when members were publicly tried and reprimanded in church, other Baptists told me, "He won't even let you see the book. He won't let it out of his hands." But he did; he even let me bring it home to do the research.

Claude has been a farmer all his life. He had one son, whose abrupt death several years ago left him even more gentle-voiced. For several years, back around 1918, he had a corn-shredding business in partnership with his father-in-law, Davey.

"The shredder was powered by a wood-burning engine," Claude said, smiling, "and Davey was one of those people who believe it's bad luck to burn sassafras. Once we were working at a little run-down farm where there wasn't much to burn. Not much of anything for anything, in fact. We had already used up all the scraps of old board and fence post we could find. Davey was feeding the corn shredder. The engine man looked around for something else to burn and saw an old, broken-down chicken trough. He was about to break it up when he noticed it was made of sassafras. He stopped for just a minute and then said to me, 'Don't you tell Davey, but I'm goin' to burn it, anyway.' He put it in the fire and it wasn't ten minutes before the shaker broke down in the furnace."

Dick confessed, "Well, now I know why I've been in trouble all winter. Last fall when the boys cut wood for the Franklin stove they cut a lot of sassafras and we've been burning it all winter."

Ignorance of the superstition may have been all that saved us from complete disaster. Even so, there were times . . . like that red cow mysteriously dying, and the mule colt drowning in the pond on Christmas night, and Dick losing his favorite log chain off of the tractor . . .

⚰ CARR AND IRIS stopped here on their way home from town and we all sat at the round table in front of the stove in the kitchen. I laid a stick of hackberry on the fire and its deep-ridged, rough bark caught immediately, sending out a burst of brass-colored sparks and the smell of nuts roasting.

Carr said, leaning forward and rubbing his big, gnarled hands together, "They say when the fire shoots out sparks like that it's going to snow."

"Snow was predicted for this evening, but maybe not for around here," Iris said. She used to teach geography in high school and always speaks precisely, in an unargumentative voice. I have never known Iris to scream or speak extravagantly, although she has had some grievous experiences. She is a generous neighbor but so easily lets herself feel obligated that about all one can give her in return is affection and listening.

"I go by the guineas," Dick said. "If they go to roost in the Bantyhouse instead of in the hedge-apple tree behind the barn, I know we're going to have falling . weather."

"Where did they go tonight?" I thought I'd had all the winter I could stand for one year.

"To the Bantyhouse."

"Oh." There is a somewhat limited range of temperature in which the human spirit is fluid, and I don't need to look at any of the thermometers to know when the temperature has dropped below or risen above it. I know because suddenly all of yesterday's exciting plans seem flat and unimportant.

Iris's prediction was right. The guineas were right. By the next morning the sky was gray, the air cold and windy, making ready for snow. Birds hurried to the feeders to fill up against the cold they knew was coming.

When I went out to the porch for an armload of wood Carr drove into the driveway and asked me his traditional joke—"Say, could you spare a feller a load of wood?"—and waited for my traditional answer.

The day they married, Carr and Iris moved into the house with Carr's parents, Clint and Eaglie. Each couple had its separate rooms, and all rooms were heated with wood-burning stoves. Eaglie cooked on a big wood-burning range in her kitchen in the log part of the house. Firewood was a vital fact of life to her, as important as Sunday shoes to wear to church, or a bin of potatoes in the cellar under the low-ceilinged, cozy living room.

The year John Dunning cleared his creek bank he cut some big trees and because he heated his house with fuel oil and his wife cooked on an electric stove, John gave the trees to Carr and Eaglie for firewood. He even helped cut them into stovewood length and hauled the wood in his wagon to the Stanger woodpile. There were eight wagon loads, a beautiful, neat wall of it. Eaglie was as proud of it as a farmer is of his new bull or a woman is of a new baby. The next time I visited her I congratulated her, just as one is expected to do in the case of a new bull or baby.

Carr said impulsively, "You come down, Rachel, and I'll give you a load of wood."

Eaglie turned to him as if she had been jabbed with

a pitchfork. "My lord, Carr, not a whole load!" she cried. That is my traditional answer to Carr's joke. It is a kind of affectionate memorial for Eaglie.

↘ NETTIE MORGAN, Hendricks County farm woman, used to tell her little daughter Mary as they walked together in the woods, "Wherever the good Lord puts a hurt, He puts a cure nearby." She pointed out wood nettles that sting mercilessly if you barely touch them, and growing near them touch-me-nots that, rubbed to a pulp, will ease the nettles' stings.

↘ ON A WINDY SPRING MORNING Eula Campbell called me, in good spirits. "My duck hatched this morning. Five eggs out of seven. Two days early. I told James this wind just blowed 'em out of the shells."

Their nine-year-old adopted daughter, Carmen, was happy also that morning because their yellow cat had just had ten kittens.

Eula went on, "You know them goose eggs Dick gave me? I put 'em under my setting goose and do you know what? She rolled 'em right out of the nest. Only them five. I don't know how she knew the difference from her own fourteen, but she sure did."

Perhaps because hers were already warmed.

The Campbell house sits back from the road and in spring the driveway breaks into soft mudholes. Driving back to the house you first pass the little shop where Jimmy repairs clocks and watches. There are always some interesting old clocks there and a few violins. Jimmy plays the "fiddle" with a square-dance group.

The Campbells always have a variety of hit-and-miss poultry; a white turkey gobbler that chases Carmen whenever he gets an opportunity; ducks and geese and one Bantam hen that lays pale-blue eggs. Eula was saving a setting of these, she said, "to set when the sign is right."

"That reminds me," I told her. "A reader has written me asking when is the right sign of the moon for her to wean her baby?"

Eula Campbell knew at once. She has never had any children of her own, but she knows the zodiac. "She should wean him when the sign is in the legs, going down. That's Aquarius, waterman. If she weans him when the sign is in the heart or breast he'll cry all the time and won't do any good."

Eula knows farm ways and folklore from having listened when she was a child. When another reader asked me, "What is a vinegar bee, does it have something to do with making bread?" I asked Eula.

"No," she said, "it has nothing to do with bread. It makes vinegar. Ask James. His mother had one once."

Jimmy said, "It was amber-colored and gelatinous. About bead size, and it grew. My mother kept it in a half-gallon glass jar of water, I think, on the back of the kitchen range. I think she put in a little sugar, too." He didn't remember how long it took, but the bee rose and sank and eventually the water turned to vinegar. "Ask Johnny Turner," he added. "His mother had one."

Johnny, ditcher and farmer, didn't remember, but his wife, Helen, remembered her mother had one. "Kind of like a sponge, about the size of a pea. You had to keep it going, like starter yeast. Mary would know."

Her sister Mary, a teachers college graduate who didn't like teaching and happily became a farmer's wife, did know, and I should have thought to ask her in the first place. Mary can make "cat's cradles" on her fingers out of pieces of string, or fold a handkerchief into "twins in a hammock" to keep a child quiet in church. She has four grandchildren.

"I remember the vinegar bee because it was my job to feed it. Every day or so you had to give it so much sugar. It made pretty good vinegar. It was kind of yeasty stuff; particles of it would go up and down and some settled on the bottom of the jar. In summer we kept it in the cellar, in winter in the kitchen. It was kind of gobby-lookin' stuff. You could make vinegar and then more vinegar."

In the scholarly Ripley-Dana *Cyclopedia*, 1880 edition, it is called vinegar plant, a name I thought less appealing than the farm name vinegar bee, and scientific directions are given for preparing it. The floating mass has much the color and texture of a piece of water-soaked glue, apparently, and the delicate, interlaced threads of its mycelium can be seen under a microscope. It is the mycelium of the same fungus that produces blue, green, or yellow mold on bread, the book says. But in the welfare state of being given food and proper temperature, the mycelium gets lazy and produces no mold. As the Ripley-Dana expresses it, "It makes no effort to reproduce itself in spores."

What makes the vinegar bee like humans is that the individual adapts itself to the environment and, where the living is easy, makes no effort to develop its own resourcefulness.

ᕙ Farmers have some unusual names for familiar objects, and in some cases the reason for the name is lost. For example, why does Fred Dutton call a dollar bill a "toadskin"?

As I walked along the road yesterday I found a toadskin on the blacktop pavement. It was flattened, stiff, dry, its essence pressed out no doubt by a car. A small, dark skin with dark splotches on its wrinkled back, and hardly thicker than a field daisy would have been, brought in and pressed for sentiment's sake between heavy books.

Among the superstitions associated with toads is the belief that it is bad luck to kill one. Probably true, for a good many crop-eating insects will thereby survive. There is no proof for the superstition that toads are poisonous to the touch. I have great respect for these creatures which as a species have been able to survive since long before man even appeared on earth. So I picked up the dry toadskin and brought it to a magnifying glass to discover if possible why it should be associated with a dollar bill. I found no reason. Unless it is that the toad's dying expression, fixed and dried on its face, could be compared to the set, grim expression on the face of the dollar bill's George Washington. The toad face expressed angry contempt. The tiny dark eye on the right side of the head (that side being uppermost revealed the toad's in right profile) was open, and bright with a baleful glare. Two tiny teeth protruded, meeting, from the firmly closed, straight line of wide mouth. Nevertheless, there was a look of dignity and courageous uncomplaint on the toad's face. Imprinted there permanently; as if, traveling without police escort or Boy Scout tenderness, the toad had said, "In God we trust." It was a small toad and must have looked very small indeed starting with nothing but trust to get across the road.

🐦 CLOVIS WEBB had left his tractor and hay baler overnight in a rented field on the old Monroe County Poor Farm, which is no longer used for the poor. The farm had become a burden to the county commissioners and they gave it into the care of the Soil Conservation Service and the S.C.S. share-rented the hayfield to Clovis. The field was fenced, but the night he left his tractor there vandals cut the fence and wrecked tractor and baler.

"They simply rimracked it," Clovis told Dick, explaining why he hadn't got the hay out of the field.

Any farmer would have known what he meant. The tractor was demolished, ruined, damaged beyond repair. Farmers regularly use words other people never knew. If the need arises they make them up of whatever is at hand, as old-time pioneers made bowls and potato mashers, lard scoops and fence-post mauls, out of wood which was plentiful, and hollowed out big poplar logs to make meat-curing tanks or horse troughs.

In this community when something costs too much farmers say, "It's pretty salty" or "I had to set the satchel down." If someone is doing him a free favor, Carr says, "I was reapin'." If you ask him an embarrassing question he pushes his cap to the back of his head and protests, "You're shootin' in the nest!" Grace Mitchell's grandfather used to say, "Maybe it won't work, but anyway I'm going to hit it a blurt."

Clovis's "rimracked" was perfectly familiar to me and when I quoted it in a newspaper column it brought a response from Claude Mahoney, newspaperman in Fairfax, Virginia.

He said, "Early in World War I, I was covering Navy for the Washington *Star*. One of my associates was Walter Logan, a young reporter from the then United Press. He was from somewhere in the Southwest and had a drawl and some good regional words. One day he wrote 'rimracked' into his copy and somehow it got past the Washington desk and onto the trunk line.

"So many inquiries came in from editors that it came to the attention of the late Lyle Wilson, then Washington UP manager. He told Walter never to use it again. It was a new word to me and I am glad to see you have brought it back."

When Kentucky-born Virgil Sims said, "The mail has run," I knew it meant it was too late to put a column into the mailbox that morning. But when Barbara Restle and Kay Turner, both New Englanders, told me significantly at a summer picnic, "It's snowing down South," I had no idea what they meant. It means your white slip is showing below the hem of your skirt. If my slip had been black or dark blue, I suppose they could have said, "The smog is simply terrible in Los Angeles this evening."

🌱 "WHAT ARE YOU DOING, Rachel?" asked my son's wife, Joyce, phoning from their home in another county where he is the District Conservationist.

"Writing a book."

"Oh, my!"

When Joyce invokes her "my" she never says what

it is a "my" of, as my sister Nina says "Oh, my goodness," or Fred Weymouth says "Oh, my country."

It is a special expressiveness Joyce has added to the family's particular vocabulary. I have never known anyone who can get more into a "my" than Joyce, who is pretty and capable, and infinitely kind. Her "my" conveys the deepest understanding of whatever situation just then needs understanding as, for example, writing a book.

Joyce's "oh, my" is as useful as a paper clip or sunglasses, or the little wad of baling twine I always have to take out of Dick's overalls pocket before I wash them.

↘ "CERTAINLY FAITH CAN move mountains," said Brink Stillwater, farmer, "but sometimes it has to do it an armload at a time."

Time and the Violets

❧ IN INDIANA we have at least nine seasons in an average year, built around an average annual growing season of 188 days. To move away from this abundance to a place that has only four seasons is like moving out of the big, rambling farmhouse you were born in to a small city apartment. Hoosiers thus moving admit homesickly, "I really prefer a change of season."

Indiana's climate is classified as mild, dispersed over early summer, real summer, unusual summer, record summer, pre-autumn, Indian summer, autumn, pre-winter, winter, spring-in-winter, deep winter, blackberry winter, sudden spring, spring-fever spring, real spring, and perfect spring.

Indiana people like having so many seasons because it gives everybody something to complain about. Whatever you ought to do that you don't want to, you can leave undone and blame it on the weather.

⩔ IN LATE WINTER every year blackbirds stream in upon the west pasture in a seemingly endless line, like a string of yarn being unraveled from a black sweater.

This late December morning they settled where the pasture was still green. There is something there they like to eat. But they were restless and kept seething up, flying a short space, settling again, regrouping and walking, moving steadily forward like soot blown before the wind. There were so many they literally covered the lower end of the pasture.

Presently the guineas and halfcocks discovered them and charged, screeching like rusty hinges being forced open. The blackbirds retreated and resettled a short distance further uphill. The defenders charged again and one peahen joined the attack.

This went on for several entertaining minutes until finally the blackbirds gave up and flew into the woods on the farm across the road, and the farm poultry subsided back to the barnlot.

Time and the Violets

🌿 THE GUINEAS ARE of three patterns: black bodies, elegantly polka-dotted with white, and throat feathers of a smoky-mauve softness; white bodies, overlaid with a filmy gray haze; some gray bodies, messily splotched with white and not very pretty.

Their small, featherless heads are covered with wrinkled skin like fine white leather, and have a peak at the top. Fat, red wattles like handlebar mustaches hang down at the sides of the beaks. An inexperienced beholder is likely to think he has only imagined guineas because no bird could really look like that. On the other hand, no imaginary bird could have such a raucous voice, or a body profile so much like a flea's, or be so instantly, acutely aware of any unusual thing going on at the farm.

🌿 WE CALL THEM halfcocks because we didn't know what else to call them. They were hatched out of guinea eggs fertilized by a peacock. The year of their hatching we had only one guinea, a lonely hen, and only one peacock, also lonely because his hen was busy sitting on a nest of her own eggs.

The guinea brooded her own eggs and hatched three chicks. One, greatly deformed, soon died. Another, with a crossed bill, survived. The third was unhandicapped. They grew to the size and almost the shape of the peahen, but lacked the Spanish comb that gives a peahen elegance. Gentle, almost timid, they have vulturous-looking heads. Their dark feathers lack the peafowl brilliance, but attractively suggest masses of dark chiffon with a green, soft light glowing above it. They have extremely harsh voices, and we never knew whether they

29

were male or female, except that the peacock sometimes preens himself before them.

They became tame, were finally accepted by the farm poultry, and seemed contented. I always threw extra portions of brown bread or hamburger to the one with the crossed bill. But one spring night a predator caught that one and ate half of it.

🐦 A FAMILY FARM is a place where everyone somehow manages to have his own way, and antipodal as the ways may be, they create a kind of unity.

One year when Joe was the Soil Conservationist in Gibson County he decided Dick and I needed peafowls on the farm. We already had Bantams, guineas, ducks, geese, horses, cattle, and mules. We had never raised peafowls and had no desire to.

Nevertheless, he bought us a cock and hen and we have never been without them since. They have added enormously to the pleasure and interest of the farm.

They are not musical. When Mark Twain said, "Italians have voices like peacocks," it was not meant as a compliment. Neither are they edible, except in India, where they originated. They produce no feathers for making mattresses or pillows, but the cocks have gorgeous trains that unfold into nine-foot fans in green, purple, blue, and bronze iridescently. In late July they begin to lose their long feathers and at that time, seeming bewildered and moody as a woman going through the menopause, they stop yelling "yowk" every time a car door slams or a teen-aged neighbor guns his motorcycle passing the farm. By early spring, they have regained both train and voice.

Their vocabulary is strange and fascinating, a low, ventriloquistic murmur, a yelp, a sharp click by which the hen warns the chicks to be mistrustful, a soft murmur by which she tells them it's safe to accept the proffered food from the outstretched human hand, and a short, sharp exclamation of curiosity. If food is not offered promptly at the kitchen door, they honk imperiously. In infancy, the chicks keep up a faraway-sounding wail that causes their Bantam foster mother to lose her sanity. But of all the peafowl vocabulary, the cock's love cry is probably the saddest and most poignant.

The chicks already have wing feathers when hatched. Their heads are slightly flattened and bright brown, their legs long and ungainly. Despite a somewhat hunched-over posture, they have a look of elegance.

The hen stole out a nest in a place across the road that seemed an open invitation to predators, so one day while she was on her food-and-water break, we took the eggs and put them under a trustworthy little Bantam in a safe nest. When the peahen returned and found the nest empty she wailed aloud. The cock went down to look and wailed with her. We resolved never to do that again, but from those eggs we got a chick that grew into Queenie.

Later that summer the hen made another nest, this one in the wildlife corner. We left it, intending to move the eggs just before hatching time. We waited one night too long; a fox killed the hen and ate half the eggs. From one of the three we gathered up and set under a Bantam, we got Dolly. She had no fear of us or of strangers and was so tame we could always pick her up and stroke the long, green-feathered throat. In winter she walked down the snowy path to the kitchen for doughnuts. When I slid the long door open she walked right in. Like any woman in a strange kitchen, she was interested in everything and walked around looking at the kitchen stove, the big green pepper plant in the stone jar, the two kitchen tables covered with red-and-white tablecloths, the flame leaping in the Franklin stove, and the two people sitting at the round table watching her.

We had been told peahens will hide their nests and you cannot possibly find them, so we were delighted when Dolly chose a nest site in plain view, on a bale of hay in the machinery shed. She sat there patiently for more than the necessary twenty-eight days, for her eggs proved to be infertile, but much of the time the young cock sat beside her, affectionately grooming her eyes, which is the way peafowls express a mutual trust.

When Queenie hatched we put her chicks in a small coop with a Bantam hen. Later that morning I discovered Queenie and the cock standing quietly outside the shed, against the wall. They stood, with heads bowed down and close together like two sorrowing parents trying to comfort each other. We gave Queenie back her chicks, and as soon as they were feathered out let them all run loose. Only one survived, but contrary to the report that peahens are poor mothers, Queenie was devoted to this one and continued to pick up food and lay it before him even after he was larger than she was.

The next spring Queenie began appearing in the barnlot for feed and water and then disappearing mysteriously, as if she had evaporated. One day Dick said, "I found Queenie's nest. It has three eggs and a hulled walnut in it."

When I walked down the road to see it, Queenie looked up at me, unafraid when I spoke to her. She had chosen her nest site wisely. Her slate and gray colors blended well with the gray sticks and leaves on the ground and the greenery sheltering the nest. The blue flowers of tall star bellflower, plumes of Solomon's-seal, wild mustard, and wild morning glories twined into elderberry bushes hid the nest and Queenie from traffic, and exploring hungry animals. It was a beautiful spot in which to spend the time brooding three eggs and a hulled walnut. The nest was never raided and, to our pleasure, Queenie even managed to bring her three chicks across the road and through the pastures to the barnlot the morning they hatched.

⩊ THE GROUND WAS frozen hard, the air sharp as a splinter from a silo stave. The late-rising sun reddened the horizon to the color of plum juice, but before it reached the springlot maple began to sulk in low-hanging, brassy gold. It was Sunday and we were eating a late breakfast when Harold Galyan arrived. One of his mares had foaled in the night and he wanted a few bales of extra good hay for her.

Harold is a horse trader. He dresses like a western cowhand . . . boots, blue jeans, denim jacket, wide-brimmed hat rolled up westernly at the sides. We were glad to see him. His conversation is always sprightly and he never repeats his stories.

Dick was embarrassed because it was after daylight and he was still at breakfast. This embarrassment is vestigial, surviving from an era when a farmer had to be up and start the morning chores "just when the crow leaves the limb." Now when most farmers have rural electricity and all the conveniences of the city, plus the country luxuries of space and privacy, many have enough powerful

33

labor-saving machinery to need a full-time maintenance man. Nearly all family farms buy milk instead of keeping a dairy cow. Actually city workers who live in the country have to get up and go to work earlier than most farmers, but this is something no farmer wants to admit. His conscience bothers him if he isn't up and doing his barn chores by daybreak.

In the horse-and-plow-farming era if a farmer was eating breakfast at eight o'clock it was because he had been up all night with lambing ewes or a sick colt. Even then he had probably fed and curried the work horses, broken the ice on the trough and watered the cattle, milked and fed the cows. Breakfast was likely to be fried ham or sausage with gravy, hot biscuits, cooked cereal with thick cream, stewed prunes or home-canned blackberries, doughnuts, and coffee. Maybe also fried eggs or fried potatoes. A syrup pitcher was always on the table, its contents called either "syrup molasses" or simply "them."

Harold was just as embarrassed as Dick, because from walking across the back yard he had snow on his high-topped leather boots. He stood on the cold back porch, with the kitchen door open and letting in cold air while he insisted, "No, I'm not coming in to track up her floor." The kitchen floor is covered with Armstrong's red-tile inlaid linoleum, easily wiped up and seldom as clean as Harold's compliment would imply. Certainly never as clean as his wife keeps the floor of their suburban kitchen.

After Harold had declined several times I took him by the hand and led him to the rocking chair by the Franklin stove. This is unorthodox, but the porch air was cold. He submitted readily to the rocker, but steadfastly refused breakfast, even a cup of coffee. There is a rule about this. When a neighbor appears at a farmer's house at mealtime and is of course invited to eat, he can get out of it by saying, "Thanks, I just got up from the table." After that the most the farmwife can press on him is a cup of coffee or a glass of buttermilk. Unless there is pie. A man can always accept a piece of pie. On the farm, pie is the great common denominator.

Harold has a small farm in this community. He tends its fields, but rents its house. His tenants are never very satisfactory. One year they were a flotsam of hippies that moved, leaving the rent unpaid, the upstairs in process of secret remodeling, and a patch of marijuana growing behind the woodshed. Harold share-crops his cornfield, keeps some fields in hay and pasture. Dick bales his hay.

His wife, Mary, is pretty, young-looking, and steadily mistrusts Harold's business judgment. "If I want to buy something she never wants me to buy it, and after I've bought it she never wants me to sell it," he says cheerfully. Tidy, nervously energetic, Mary is the kind of housekeeper who can't sit in front of an open fire without poking it.

Their only child, a daughter, is married and lives in Colorado. Her two children are the joy of Harold's life. He would like to move to Colorado.

But he believes in disciplining the grandchildren. Once, starting to spank the five-year-old, he was promptly bitten on the leg by the three-year-old. The surprise of it "stopped me cold as a Christian's heart." Unintentionally and in love, they got revenge, one summer evening when their mother was going out. She left them with Harold and they went to bed with him. One climbed in on each side of him and, being much lighter, rolled in against him. "I couldn't turn over and I couldn't go to

35

sleep," he said. "They were like little furnaces and when Susan got back I told her, 'Get these kids out of here.' "

He sat in the rocking chair while we finished breakfast. In the pleasure of the visit both men forgot their embarrassment; I got material for a farm column and the day got off to a good start for everyone, including Harold's mare. She got a breakfast of first-class alfalfa hay. "It's so good," Dick told Harold, "I only feed it on Sundays and holidays."

❧ THE RASPBERRY PATCH is a kind of winter trampoline for birds. This morning I watched a sparrow fly down onto a high springy curve of purple cane. It vibrated, and he rode up and down on it. When the vibration stopped, he rose up and came down again, hard, to set it going again, apparently just for the fun of it.

❧ "HOW CAN YOU STAND IT?" I asked Dick as he was getting ready to go out and do the morning chores at the barn. Snow had fallen in the night. The sun was only a pink blob on the horizon like a smear of fruit on a plate that has been washed and ought to be clean.

"You jist take a look at that pile of clothes I put on when I go out," he answered, picking up a tall felt boot and knocking the chaff out of it. There was a hooded wool jacket, a quilted jacket, a cap with fur-lined ear muffs, a pair of denim overalls, the tall boots, and a piece of bailing twine to tie around his waist because, as his Uncle Howard taught him, "It's equal to another jacket."

I said, "Oh, I don't mean that. I mean this perpetual gray, this winterness going on forever . . ."

"It's all in the spirit," he said. "If you have some way to keep your spirit up . . ."

"Well, what's your way?"

"You look at the calves and think how nice they are and what you're going to do with them . . . or the fields . . . or the mule colts. If you have something you like to think of you don't have to think, 'How can I set this foot out in that cold snow?' " He put on one boot. "My feet haven't been really warm since last August," he admitted. Then he put on his other boot and wrapped his spirit around him and set his foot out in the cold snow.

⟍ GRAFFITO, WEBSTER SAYS, is "a rude inscription, figure, drawing, etc., found on rocks, walls, vases, and other objects."

That's human graffito, done with hands. Foot graffito is done by animals, in snow, mud, or soft rock that hardens and holds the message to be delivered thousands of years later. Animal graffito is brief and functional, and never obscene.

Tuesday's snow provided perfect graffito surface. Snow fell all day out of gray curtains, sometimes hissing against the house wall, sometimes drifting hurriedly, like a cloud, past the hilltop woods. By night it was four inches deep. The full moon glowed under lampshade clouds as if it had only one night to empty itself of light.

Snow thickened in pristine softness on shed roofs, cistern pump, woodpile, parked car, and all the trees. It whitened the spirea bush at the end of the walk and the rosebush by the porch window. Security lights that are usually a glare in the horizon were whittled down to mere stars. The night was magical, luminous, the kind of night on which something unforgettable might occur. Waking, I walked from window to window, delighted. If I had been a shepherd tending my flock on a hillside I could easily have heard angels singing and the song would certainly have been something like "Fear not," for when the earth speaks of creation it speaks reverently, without fear.

Wild creatures must have felt the night, too. In the moonlight a rabbit came out and wrote one terse line of graffito. A long, thin line, rigidly disciplined and in a code made of two small back footprints and one long front footprint together, repeated at regular intervals all the way across the yard, curving finally, down into the wildlife corner.

But the next morning, seeing the whole blank page of east yard lying unused, the rabbit may have felt he had been too laconic. He came again and under a morning sun more pale than the night's moon, gave free expression to his writing impulses. He wrote in forked paths, dancings, crisscrossing lines that obliterated each other. The writing made no mention of food or escape. It was pure revelry, graffito at its gayest, most expressive rabbitness.

🦅 A BLACK-SPOTTED, orange-colored ladybug was walking on the rim of the sink when I came to wash dishes. Briskly, as if someone had told her, "Your house is on fire; your children will burn." This beetle, of the family Coccinellidae, is recognized as a gardener's friend, so I brushed it onto a paper and carried it outdoors, wishing I could stay there myself instead of in the kitchen painting a wall.

The ladybug's timing was understandably poor. Last fall during Indiana's lovely, colored-leaf indolence, it had gone into hibernation in a niche of the woodpile, among leaves deposited there by wind. Winter's unseasonable cold had eroded the woodpile faster than in normal years and the ladybug therefore awoke yesterday in the dusty, warm woodbox of a kitchen reeking of paint and faced with another legislative time change.

It may have been one of the hundreds that appeared suddenly last fall on the front wall of the house, on porch floor, on flowerpots, and on all the porch furniture. They seemed to be all moving slowly toward some chosen destination. I left them undisturbed and within two days they had vanished completely.

In the natural world the ladybug beetle is one of the props that upholds the natural balance, preying voraciously on aphids, scale insects, and garden pests. Some garden seed catalogues even offer ladybugs for sale, along with weed killers, legume encouragers, and other garden aids. The appetite that makes the ladybug as beneficial as the praying mantis in the garden probably also makes it a creature of terror in its own insect world. Perhaps in the world of greenflies, aphids, and scale insects the ladybug occupies the place humankind occupies in the wildernesses.

It is likely the ladybug's life is dependent on its voraciousness, just as a shrew's life depends on its catching and eating several times its own weight in insects every day.

My ladybug guest, waking in the woodbox to discover it had already lost an hour on account of Indiana's legislature moving the clocks up an hour, might feel the loss of the time and therefore be in a hurry to get on with the predation.

I gathered it up on a piece of cardboard, then took time to examine it under a magnifying glass. Given time and a common language in which to discuss it, the beetle and I would probably agree that the raw material of time is change. It is the creative tool by which evolution is accomplished, and by which the insect has become a black-spotted orange beetle and my species has become a two-legged animal with hands and large brain. If nothing changed, time would stand still. Man and insect would alike be static, motionless forever like ancient insects immersed in prehistoric amber.

The beetle walked to the edge of the cardboard, insistently. Perhaps it was uncomfortable under my magnified scrutiny. If insects, being much smaller than humans, are able to see more of the small details of their surroundings, they probably see humans as large and terrifying creatures. The power of the human gaze, which I have discovered is disquieting to birds, especially when aided by a field glass, is probably distressing to insects. To the ladybug the human eye may be a mountain-sized, light-bearing lens, full of menace.

I had to hurry back to my kitchen-painting. The beetle, finding itself once more close to the comfortable, familiar elements, crumb of earth and fragment of old leaf, quickly vanished when I set it down.

Time is something people take for granted, wish they had more of, complain they never have any of for themselves, and waste as if they had flowing wells of it in their back yards. Actually what makes time scarce or abundant is not so much the hour, as what the hour is leading into. This much the ladybug and I mutually understood as we hurried to our separate urgencies.

🌱 ON THE FARM now the ice age is over, the glaciers have melted. The landscape, swathed in thin gray light, is splotched with patches of primordial ooze. A great deal of the glacial waters ran off before the hard-frozen ground could absorb it.

Late winter rains have softened the bleached-brown pasture sod like hot syrup poured over buttered pancakes, and in some unprotected farms it seems almost too fragile to survive even the loud sounds of traffic. Livestock must be kept out until the ground settles and grass roots have toughened.

In the poultry yards mud stands in shallow places, like creamed coffee poured into saucers to cool. Ducks sip eagerly from these saucers, but when they have to cross a field they fly rather than paddle through the mud. Even the geese, inherently able to awkwardize everything they do, prefer to fly. In flight, big and white and dramatic-looking, they are called a "skein"; on the ground they are a "gaggle." The difference in appearance is as great as the difference in words.

Surely the earth was never more beautiful, even when blossoming or when autumn-colored, than now when the familiar green-and-brown surface is newly disclosed. All the farm stock rejoice. Cattle stand by the barn, soaking up the sunlight.

This perhaps is how it was eons ago when the glaciers melted and animals began to wander into new places, and earth was reshaping. The farm now is a miniature reconstruction of earth remembering its formative beginnings, when seas were receding, mountains were being pushed up, and new plants and animals were developing.

Now the lichens on stones and tree trunks turn bright green. Moss on the ground grows plushy and bright and tiny fronds rise out of it. Even the woodpile is bright, and when I go to get a stick to burn I am reluctant to burn the beauty of old, bare elm or the gnarled root of peach. In this era birds appear on earth and reptiles also.

On these mornings it is obvious to the whole farm-earth that any time now man will appear. He will begin to tame, feed, and use the animals and confine them in places where he prefers them to be. He will walk uprightly across the muddy stretches and the few remaining ice patches. He will wade through water, admire and calculate the worth of new grass, and estimate how soon the cattle can be let out on it. Presently he will make his way to his desk in the house and fill out his income-tax returns. Machinery will roar, progress will set in for better or worse, and earth will be at the mercy of this two-legged newcomer.

꙼ BUZZARDS RETURN to Indiana in mid-March and we welcome them for their services on the highways. These scavengers will find many little feasts of wildlife and domestic pet on our ever-growing, ever-hastening roads.

For wildlife, fear is a defensive weapon. Now that most small creatures, rabbits, squirrels, possums, skunks, raccoons, and birds have become accustomed to the sight and sound of motor vehicles, many have lost their fear. The result is a heavy death toll.

When I went to the mailbox today I found a possum lying dead in the road. Apparently he was killed at one swift blow. I think I knew him. I have seen a possum running incautiously along this road several times. This morning he lay on his side composedly, his feet neatly placed in pairs like patient little hands together. I carried him to the side of the road, which is beginning to be green now. The returning buzzards with their telescopic sight will see him there, from their high paths in the sky, and will know what to do about it.

🌿 THE EARLY-MORNING WIND ran downhill singing of spring. At the wildlife corner of the front yard it pushed through slits in the tops of maple and locusts, turning them into a woodwind section of its orchestra. It ran on up to the front porch and shook the solemn clay windbell at the roof's edge and the bell answered, measuring the wind in its earthy utterances.

The whole day was musical.

A mockingbird came to the back yard, where snow had melted in the night and collected into a tiny pool. The elegance of its sipping made me thirsty. I had been reading Lewis and Clark's *Journal*, and as I watched the mockingbird sip I thought ironically that although travel was hard and dangerous in 1804–06, when the two explorers searched for an overland route to the Pacific, and their medical supplies were crude, and some of the Indians were hostile, nevertheless they could safely drink from any clear-running stream or pool they came to. Modern travelers cannot do that, and that morning I was

43

not even sure it was safe for the mockingbird to sip the clear snow water.

In the evening, remembering I had left my jacket at the barn, I went up to get it. The air was cool and damp and had the smell and taste of spring. The early-evening moon hung low in the sky like a lantern hanging from a peg in the barn when a farmer is doing his chores late. The wind snatched up masses of dark cloud like armloads of dark chiffon and threw them across the face of the moon and the moon's brilliance turned them to gold. I could see my own shadow following me up to the barn. The stones of the back walk were wet and in the moonlight they shone like little pools of water. It was as if, reversing the way of land creatures, some clever little water animal had built itself a bridge of little pools, by which, step by step, he could get across the dry land.

⍦ EVERY FAMILY NEEDS its backlogs of jokes by which to warm its heart through the bleak times, and its special vocabulary and proverbs that grow from shared experiences. These are heirlooms, individualized and handed down like the monogrammed coin silver teaspoons. They are a manifestation of what Robert Louis Stevenson in his prayer calls "the love that unites us, the hope with which we expect the morrow."

They are practical, too. As a code, a family's special language can explain a situation briefly and avoid much argument.

I came in from the not quite warm midmorning and heard a rustling as of dresser drawers being raked through, closets being searched, doors being hopefully opened and shut, and the laundry hamper being cross-examined, and I knew Dick was hunting something.

His hunting-something sound is like no other sound. It is most penetrating when he is going through old cigar boxes where he keeps his business papers for income-tax returns. This time, though, I had the feeling it was not tax papers, or pliers, or the movie camera he was looking for, and I offered to help. He said piteously, "I can't find that last suit of long-handled underwear I saved and this thermal stuff is too hot today."

All farm women know that garment called "long underwear." A one-piece cotton pelt that was intended to give warmth and probably did when it was new and its inside was fleecy. It buttoned down the front and at critical places in the back, but invariably the buttons departed from it and the buttonholes stretched beyond caring. After several years of wearing and washing, the knees bagged obscenely and sometimes broke into open wounds. The neckband, snug-fitting at first, eventually stretched to waist circumference. In the proper chest size, the legs were always too short for a tall man and pulled out from the tops of his socks. His wife had to cut off tops of a pair of work socks and sew them onto the underwear leg cuffs for proper length. The sleeve cuffs lost their elasticity, ripped open, and were always able to work their way through the shirt-sleeve placket at mealtime and there hang like a white flag or drag across the dinner plate.

On the day when modern technology presented farmkind with thermal underwear I gave thanks and happily cut up the last pelt into dust cloths and silver-polishing rags for which the garment is supremely adapted. At the moment of Dick's piteous hunting cry, the last long-handled underwear pelt was only a proud stack of polishing cloths, neatly folded and put away on the cleaning-supply shelf.

I could have joined deceitfully in the search and thus avoided confessing. But a man is entitled to the truth about his underwear. It is one of America's freedoms, and the duty of the press and all people serving the press is to help keep these freedoms inviolate.

I couldn't bear to say, "I cut it up into little pieces," so I used the family code. I said, "I think the Lord has called that underwear home."

Dick understood. He accepted. He closed the dresser drawer and said only, "I wish I could ever be around here when the Lord comes calling for things. I'd like to do some business with Him."

THIS IS THE WAY the last snow went off: At noon the world was glaring in harsh white. An hour later there was a hint of brown on the sloping hillsides, like a dish towel beginning to wear thin. Then the rain came and rinsed away the snow like soapsuds. It brightened the lichened maple trunks. Rain brings out greenness there just as the wind brings redness to human cheeks and noses, for in the plant world the color of life is green.

The air was mild after the rain and I went out to rake away leaves that had been blown in around the red-raspberry canes last fall. Red-raspberries propagate by furry, breakable new shoots springing up from underground. A too thick covering of leaves smothers out the new shoots.

46

Last fall's leaves, now old and limp and brown, had a blossomy smell as I raked them out with my bare fingers. There were enough to fill a bushel basket several times. I dumped them over the fence into the springlot and the cattle hurried up, full of curiosity, and began to eat as if all winter they had been craving old, dead, maple leaves.

With the leaf-covering gone, the knobby, pale-green roots of violets were exposed. They grow near the surface as if they could hardly wait to push their early, heart-shaped leaves into attention. The roots look like some kind of vegetable, dyed pale-green and already slightly nibbled by rabbits.

⋎ BY EARLY SPRING violets have practically taken the yard. When we moved to this farm they were already well established in the grassy bank along the road and bearing darkly purple-blue flowers on long stems among the grass. When they began to creep up the bank and into the front yard, as wild plants do when they find congenial foothold and foodhold, we encouraged them. Dick even fertilized them lightly one spring.

Eventually they crossed the yard and went into the red-raspberry patch and on into the vegetable garden, through the black-raspberry rows, and on up into the barnlot.

Every year they come on ahead of the grass, carpeting the whole yard with their heart-shaped leaves and face-like blue flowers. We leave them alone, giving them their hour of glory, until the grass is tall enough to hide them, and by then the yard is ragged as a worn-out apron. Then we mow. But the violets are not discouraged. All summer

47

they keep making new small leaves, and the next spring they come up again, forgiving and beautiful.

When I was a child I once dreamed of visiting an old man and woman whose small house was carpeted, all over, with living violets. They grew so tall and dense you could walk on them without crushing them. The dream was pleasant and so vivid it has remained in my memory with the force of a real experience. I love violets, partly for the sake of the dream, but more because they remind me of my daughter, Carol.

When Carol lived at home she mowed the yard. She used a big, cumbersome power mower that had a side cutter bar, a big steel roller to flatten the grass, an obstinate disposition, and no reverse gear. If it got into a ditch it had to be lifted out by people. If it ran against a tree it had to be manually lifted free of it. It seldom got to indulge in these tantrums, however, because Carol, like most farm girls, was skillful with machinery. She enjoyed mowing the yard and extended its mowed boundaries up to the barn and across the barnlot.

The yard was her place of authority. She tolerated my ideas about it purely out of love of me. The tangled place at the front yard where I planted dogwood, flowering almond, and blackberries, and under the shelter of these set bleeding heart and many weeds and woods plants, and nature aided me by contributing many additional kinds of vines and weeds—all this I fondly called "the wildlife corner." Carol, mowing up to the rim of it, briskly called it "the mess."

In the wet time of year water runs in the rim. Next to the rim is the place where we have buried our dead pets, including Rose the beloved Collie, and all the songbirds and such pitifuls we found dead.

48

Carol forbade trucks or farm machinery to drive across the mowed yard. She kept it neatly mowed, but for my sake every spring she left little patches of violets unmowed, all over the yard.

Finally one day when the grass had concealed the violets and the yard had, in truth, begun to look superbly unkempt, Carol said firmly, "The violets have got to go." It became a family proverb. The summer grew older and turned its attention to other things, and the people did also. The mowed violets waited, their roots ready to come again the next spring.

The years also stacked up and Carol went away into the far Southwest to attend graduate school and then to work on a newspaper. One year she became engaged to a newspaper reporter there who had never been on a farm. The next spring Paul and Carol came home to the farm to be married. It was April and the violets were just well in bloom, dark, tall, numerous, and beautiful. The remembered aspects of home overwhelmed Carol and she got out the lawnmower, a new one by this time, smaller and more manageable, because nobody else could manage her old one. She mowed the yard, leaving big patches of blooming violets in prominent places in the front yard. She mowed happily until finally we had to stop and go into town on some wedding errand.

In our absence, Paul, loving and happy and wanting to be helpful, got out the mower and finished the yard, cutting down all the violet patches Carol had left. When she came home and saw the devastation she wept. She wept for the violets, and for herself and her childhood memories, and for Paul, who in his contrition would have been willing to go out and wire the flowers back into place.

The violets were a symbol of what Thomas Wolfe

must have meant when he said, "You can't go home again."

It was a comfort then to remember and remind Carol of the corollary to the family proverb. "The violets have got to go. But they will return."

🐦 "MAN WANTS but little here below," quoted Brink Stillwater, this being one of his favorite quotations, "but wants a lot of that little."

Things of Gold

🕊 Unwinding a wild sweet-potato vine from a lily stalk in the east yard, I discovered two tiny nuggets of pure, shining gold. They were beetles, the size and shape of a ladybug, and close together on a leaf. Their goldness was genuinely breathtaking. I took time to gasp, then broke off the long, pointed leaf on which they were cling-

ing, and holding it all loosely between my palms, carried
it to the house. I had to push open two doors with an
elbow, and reach up into a cupboard for a glass jar in
which to put my treasures, and by the time I had maneu-
vered the jar into position, one beetle was gone.

I went back over the way I had come, searching
carefully, but could not find the lost gold, and when I returned to my remaining beetle it was no longer gold, but
only orange-red. Its carapace appeared to be covered with
a transparent plastic mold extending slightly beyond the
orange-red rim, all around.

So were these beetles gold only when mating or
feeding, or at large in outdoor air and sunlight? Could
they change color at will, or were they, like peacocks, a
different color according to the angle at which light falls
on them? Now only a large splotch of iridescent blue
gleamed at the juncture of wing and forecase, no gold at
all.

I set the lid loosely on the jar and left it in sunlight
by the window. Presently the beetle had turned back to
gold and remained gold most of the time thereafter, which
eventually became several weeks. He also ate more holes
in his leaf and within the next three days ate holes in three
more leaves I brought him.

This is the first time I have known any good to come
of this vine which is also called bindweed and is a scourge
in the raspberry patch, where it wraps itself around the
canes and pulls them down before the berries can ripen in
sun. The leaves are glossy, green, and of a stretched-out
heart shape. The white morning-glory blossoms are also
attractive, opening out of long pods that resemble Japa-
nese lanterns strung up for a party. If it were more rare,
the vine would be more loved.

Things of Gold

Under the microscope the gold beetle is even more spectacular, an example of nature's extravagant use of beauty and miracle in places not likely to be seen. Two pure gold, shining wings cover the beetle's back, meeting at the center in a tight, straight line, thus creating the shield which is characteristic of Coleoptera. At the juncture a metallic blue splotch sometimes glows, and from time to time the body swathes itself mysteriously in a metallic blue glow. The curved halves of carapace are marked with tiny indentations, in meticulously even rows as if the wings had been nailed on with tiny gold nails. The gold profile of the carapace is carved on the outside into minute scallops. To design a thing more exquisite would be impossible. Most of the time my beetle stayed under his leaf, eating more round holes into it. A splendid and uncostly pet. But I still regretted the loss of the other one, and this was probably pure human greed.

I had hoped to be able to keep the beetle through winter and planned to pot a wild sweet-potato vine so I could grow leaves in the house. But late in the summer, whether from neglect on my part or because he had lived out his allotted time, the beetle grew sluggish, turned a dark color, and died.

Continuing my research, I was able to identify it as a member of the Carabidae family, in which the change of metallic color is a way of reflecting heat rays from the beetle's surface, to shield it from a too high temperature.

My respect for the natural world and the laws by which it operates increases with every new discovery of this kind. To me it is evidence of some supreme law or truth which human intelligence has not yet discovered or even come near identifying. But the search for it is a magnificent and absorbing adventure.

ᴡ "Do you remember how your home town celebrated Memorial Day when you were a little boy . . . only it was called Decoration Day then?" a woman asked Dick. His home town was Spencer, a small White River town, the county seat of Owen County.

He replied eagerly. "Oh, yes. There was always a parade. It kind of assembled in front of the courthouse. All the lodges marched in it, the Odd Fellows, Red Men, Elks, Knights of Pythias. I think the Masons marched, too, but I'm not sure. I don't remember seeing those big plumed headpieces.

"People walked, or rode horses. There was always a fife-and-drum corps, and a band. The band music was exciting. I used to watch the parade and always resolve that the next year . . . next year for sure . . . I was going to ride Old Ginger, our driving mare, in it. It was a boy's dream, you know; I never did it.

"The parade marched down the main streets and out to Riverside Cemetery. There were little flags on the veterans' graves. There were still a good many Civil War veterans then. Uncle Stanley Mead was one. The veterans all dressed up in their blue uniforms and marched in the parade; it was a big day for them. Their uniforms always filled me with a sad, nostalgic yearning; the Civil War seemed so long ago and past. And the World Wars hadn't set in yet, you know.

"The parade wound up at the cemetery and somebody always read the Gettysburg Address. And there was usually some speaking. Sam Ralston spoke once when he was running for governor or already elected. At the last the band always, always played 'Tenting on the Old Campground.' It was quite a thing, sung softly, with all those Civil War uniforms around and little flags on the graves. Everyone was pretty patriotic in those peaceful days.

"Of course we had great-uncles and grandfathers that had been in the war and told us little boys about it. Like Uncle Stanley, who was in Andersonville prison when the spring miraculously began to flow and supply drinking water to the Northern prisoners. Uncle Stanley always said it was no miracle at all; that the vein of water was already there and the weight of so many prisoners caused it to break through the ground in a weak spot."

Stanley Mead was only fourteen years old, not as tall as the bayonet tip on his rifle, when he ran away from home to join the Army. He was the color bearer. Afterward, his Army experience was always the highlight of his life. He lived in a house on steep Hillside Avenue and made his big, wooded yard into a bird sanctuary. His eyes were bright blue and he wore a short, pointed white beard that gave a look of distinction to his face. He was gentle, never seemed warlike or hate-driven. His daughter Jessie taught school in Spencer.

"When I was a little girl," said Sylvia, "people decorated the graves with home-grown roses and irises and peonies, usually in glass fruit jars. Sometimes in the little country cemeteries they decorated the graves with those old-time mustard jars that were shaped like hens and made of milk glass. They're valuable antiques now. Nobody bothered them and they gave the graves a remembered look after the flowers had withered."

Now the many artificial flowers in cemeteries give color the year round, almost a look of festival. They are better now than the first ones, which seemed only to emphasize the absence of life, but they still somewhat dispel the sense of quietness. In the little country cemeteries long grass grows and dewberry briers creep across the ground, and stiff yucca lilies bloom there in summer. Now, with power mowers available, most of the little remote places even are kept mowed. In many of them the American Legion every year puts little new flags on the graves of all veterans, and takes away last year's limp, faded ones.

↯ LAST YEAR, when the pond froze over, the mallards began to leave the farm. There was a sad dignity about their going. Perhaps they had conferred in secret; perhaps they didn't need to confer. One cold morning, realizing there was no longer any open water on the farm, they simply rose in groups of eight to twelve and flew away. Probably their wild instincts told them where to look for open water. It was an exceptionally cold winter.

↯ THEY NEVER ALL LEAVE, and some return later. Some other wild ones come, recognizing this as a place of refuge.

"I saw twenty wild mallards come down on the pond this morning," Dick said at noon one winter day. "They didn't circle and come down deliberately as they usually do. They just fluttered in and dropped as fast as they could. A hawk was after them. They know they're safe on the water; if a hawk grabbed one all the duck would have to do is dive under. The hawk knows it, too. He flew off. He flies astonishingly high."

↯ BASICALLY THE FARM-HATCHED, farm-fed mallards are wild birds, descended from a setting of eggs a soil conservationist gave Joe several years ago. The farm mallards are free to leave if they wish.

There is probably no farm creature more appealing than a mallard duckling. When they hatch, in an unprotected nest, the duck takes them immediately to the pond if she can. There, swimming behind her, they look like a fleet of tiny boats following a large one. They are easy prey for turtles and other predators or unfavorable weather, so we try to catch them and keep them in the battery until they are full-feathered. This much interference with nature seems essential to the survival of farm poultry.

Most of the farms in this community have quit raising any poultry and therefore are not as much visited by poultry predators as this one is. The mallards, evidently aware of this, sometimes nest beside the neighbors' ponds and bring their ducklings back here the day they are hatched, across the cornfields, and through the hedges. One hatched last year near Ira's pond, which is shallow and sometimes dries up in summer. She obviously liked being a big duck in a small puddle because every day she brought her ducklings to the barn here for feed and took them back to Ira's pond afterward. "I met them going back as I went down to Ira's to feed the steers," Dick said one day. "I pulled off to the side so they wouldn't have to get out of the way of the tractor, and threw them a handful of corn. We looked at each other awhile and then I went on."

EVERY YEAR I keep a few ducklings in a box in the kitchen as long as possible. They have different calls by which they ask for the different things they want, food, water, or clean papers on the box floor.

When they are big enough we put them out on grass, in a fence ring, in daytime and bring them back in at night. They become completely tame and friendly and when schoolchildren visit the farm in April and May the ducklings are an attraction to feed or pet. Young ducks have a high body temperature; against your bare arm their bodies feel almost as if they had fever. In the kitchen a pet duck would follow a farmwife eagerly, its big orange-colored feet pattering across the linoleum and making the sound of rain on summer leaves.

When the last pet duckling is feathered out and can be put out with the others, it soon integrates with the flock. One way you know summer is more than half gone is that all the different hatchlings have merged into one flock. They have their adult feathers by then; the drakes have the dark shine on their necks that will later be green. By the time they are all feathered out the late-hatched ducklings look just as old as the early-hatched ones.

IN EARLY APRIL the mallards pair off. The females walk about, exploring the ground as if they had never seen it before, tasting the little threads of water, inquiring into clumps of consider-lilies, weeds, or deep grass that might be able to conceal a duck's nest. They riffle through piles of old, winter-faded leaves as if they realized that their own black-and-brown bodies, sitting on a nest of those leaves, would be almost invisible, especially after it was lined with feathers pulled from the duck's own body. The drakes follow like mechanical toys wound up and automatically following. Their colors shine like new garments. They wear dark glowing brown, iridescent blue-green, gray, and touches of white. This week after rain had erased the last of the snow, the mallards walked out in the east pasture, sieving fresh rainwater through their wide, flat, yellow bills. Their performance was like a ballet; they went in single file, all making the same gestures simultaneously. Each took one step, ducked a yellow bill into the water, raised the head, and stepped again, all in unison, charmingly, as in a dance routine.

⌄ FINALLY THE MALLARDS make their hopeful nests all over the place . . . behind a clump of wild mustard beside the silo, under the lilies at the back walk, on a pile of old leaves against the living-room wall, on a bale of hay in the barnloft, under the workbench in Dick's workshop. We find the nests and hope the predators will not. Sometimes, for protection, we move eggs and duck into the poultry battery. Many of the nests are destroyed just before the eggs are due to hatch, for mallards have no strong defense. All they can do is ruffle up their feathers threateningly, spread out their tails into a fan, and hiss, and peck ineffectively with flat bills. I don't know how any survive in their completely unprotected wild state, but in nature's admirable and inscrutable way, enough do survive to keep the species going.

⌄ ONE OF MY deepest garden satisfactions is to go back in the evening and look at what I've done that day. From having combined my energy, sweat, and scratches with the garden's resistance and promise, I feel a companionship with earth, which is better than mastery or even equal partnership.

So I went back at evening to look at the raspberry

patch where all afternoon I had pruned and raked the pruned-off canes into windrows for burning. My orchardist father taught me to burn old raspberry canes to prevent disease overtaking new ones. I love this earthy work which is my reward for faithfulness to the house or typewriter. I had not intended to spend the whole afternoon at it, but, having started, was unable to stop until the job was finished and the day was gone. Now two long windrows lay waiting for a match and a windless day. Supper was over. I had rested; the raspberry patch had rested. We were glad to commune and I was glad to watch how evening overtakes the farm.

The sun's setting light had left a ragged pink-orange swish across a pale-blue sky. Two peacocks, wearing their new trains, came down the path past the lilac bushes now heavy with buds. Sometimes, in daylight peacock blue is an acidulous blue-green, akin to the sourness of a never-ripe plum, but in the dusklight it was a tranquil blue, gentled with gold.

In the east pasture across the fence two young black steers playfully butted their heads together, and one walked slowly down to the shallow water for a last drink. Geese also walked there solemnly, pretending not to see me. The gray ones were almost invisible against the dusk, but the white ones gleamed up distinctly. Three of them have started nests in the toolshed now, but none stays on the nest overnight.

Guineas had already gone to roost in the high open windows of the toolshed, but in their acute watchfulness they saw me and began a loud potrack-potracking. All afternoon while I worked in the raspberry patch they had expressed curiosity and disapproval by their potracking, until I drove them away with a clod.

In the barnlot one mallard walked alone and palely loitering, either returning to a nest or just leaving one to go to the pond for the night. Now that the ducks have chosen partners, some ducks have two or three partners but several partners have no duck.

The Bantams had already retired into the Bantam house and Dick had fastened their door. As the light diminished there was a feeling of finish and achievement all over the place.

🦢 THE SPIRIT of independence manifested by many weeds is as appealing as their bloom. If you dig up some of these and bring them to the security of your garden, transplanting them into places duplicating the places in which you captured them, giving thought to light, shade, moisture, kind of soil, angle of wind exposure, security from grazers, and a necessary amount of privacy, and also if you make them welcome with drinks of water and mulches around their feet until they get accustomed to the new place, they often survive. But chances are, when you look for them the next summer, they will be gone, having moved on to a place they like better. And the reason they like it better is they chose it themselves.

The black-eyed Susans I planted inside a brick-bordered flowerbed last summer were not there this year. I discovered them some distance away, beyond the pink spirea. Star bellflower, a tall, sparsely leaved plant that bears lovely blue flowers, did not stay where I planted it beside painted daisies, but went outside the fence the first year and the next year had moved around the corner of the house and out into the red-raspberry patch. There its color makes my heart rejoice like the blacksmith's who heard his children singing in the village choir mentioned by Longfellow. Red catchfly moved out across the west yard and, when it wished, stopped near the biggest maple. At breakfast Dick exclaimed, "What is that beautiful red flower? It wasn't there when I mowed the yard last week." He was right; its roots were there but it had grown tall and bloomed in those few days. That ability by which, when necessary, a wild plant can grow, bloom, and produce seeds in shortened time, is one of the unexplained and admirable talents of wild things. Or they hide somehow and reappear mysteriously. The chicory I planted in the yard a long time ago was gone for several years and this year suddenly was blooming in the east yard, which had been mowed only a week before. Normally two feet tall, this chicory was only four inches tall, but its bright-blue, asterlike flowers were of normal size.

From time to time new weeds and grasses appear in the vegetable garden, which has been tilled for many years. Seeds of jimson, butterweed, velvetleaf, bull nettle, cocklebur, burdock, wild mustard, and many others can live half a hundred years or longer deep down in the ground, waiting until after many spring plowings bring them to the top again, whereupon they sprout readily.

🌱 IN THE STRAWBERRY PATCH one year I discovered Venus's looking glass, also called mirrorweed. It was new to me and had never appeared in the garden before, and was so attractive I left it. The scalloped, shell-shaped leaves are graduated in size from a penny-big one nearest the ground to a tiny one at the plant's tip, and are all strung along the stalk without benefit of stem. Botanists call this sessile. At the juncture of stalk and leaf, one small, vividly purple-blue flower rises. I left one plant that summer and from that there was an abundance of Venus's looking glasses. But never such multitudes as to endanger the strawberries.

Weeds are not always so considerate. Waterleaf, which I never really wanted in the first place, just appeared one year in the wildlife corner. It is also called rule-of-five, which is appropriate because it is dominated by fives. The leaves, shaped like geranium leaves dusted with blight, are divided into five points, some even into five panels. The pale lilac-blue, cuplike flowers have five petals and when these have fallen, a five-pronged star-shaped calyx remains, green-white at the center. The foot-high watery green stalks with their hairy covering are ridged into five sides. And finally, this plant spreads five times as fast as you can believe even with help.

Blooming in May, it is pretty and symmetrical, but somehow uncouth in its hairiness and insipid in the same way pale-blue eyes look insipid under colorless lashes and eyebrows.

Waterleaf spreads by furry seeds, to leap across astonishing distances and appear abundantly in places where you don't want it. It should stay in the woods, where in season there is space and use for it. There, in great patches, it gives the woods an attractive sweep of blue. A class of children, visiting our hilltop woods one spring, happily brought down handfuls of waterleaf to take home. In their small hands the plants hung down limply like a dead chicken. They hoped it would revive and take root when they planted it at home and I could tell them honestly that I thought it probably would.

🐦 Suddenly today nasturtiums are in bloom. The way this came about I can't expect anybody to believe. Nevertheless, it is bedrock fact.

Every year I plant nasturtiums in memory of my mother, who liked and grew them. She kept little bouquets of different flowers in the house, often two or three on the same table. For vases she used dishes, glass canning jars, old bowls, jelly glasses, sometimes even bona fide vases. Flowers grew well for her and she often sent mailings of honeysuckle, love-in-a-mist, dahlias, or others, moistly packed in boxes, to children and friends.

When she lived on an orchard farm and her children were small, she planted red cannas and elephant's-ear in big brown tiles, like a couple of vases in the front yard. She grew scarlet sage and cornflower and hollyhocks and lilies. One spring she had no more room for planting hollyhock seed, so she took them along the highway and, as she said, "just gave them a toss." A few years later, to the astonishment of the highway mowers, they were in bloom and she persuaded the men to leave them.

This spring I planted nasturtiums at the front edge of the garden, where I hoped to see them often. They came up, made good stalk growth, but gave no hint of bud. The flat green parasols of leaf rose from crooked pale-green stems and reminded me always of a pile of rumpled clothes dampened and ready to be ironed. It was pretty and interesting and the leaves are said to be good in sandwiches if you are out of lettuce, but I wanted flowers.

So I gave the nasturtiums a good talking to, reminding them of the wheelbarrowloads of "barnyard gold" I had brought to them, and buckets of water carried in drought time, and the mulchings of yard cuttings. For all this kindness, I reminded them, they owed me flowers.

Two days later they were in bloom. Abundantly, in color tones ranging from pale-pale yellow, through striped orange-yellow, orange, peach, brown, red, and flame. A bouquet of them, in an old glass pitcher of taffy-candy pattern, has all the bright colors of a leaping, open fire. With another bouquet in the matching sugar bowl, the nasturtiums remind me of my mother's bouquets. Every time I send a clutch of nasturtiums home with a guest, it is a gift to my mother and gives me pleasure. As if to say, "You asked for it," the nasturtiums continue to bloom so lavishly they need picking every day. Unpicked, they go to seed. The pale, ridged seeds, shaped somewhat like tiny clenched fists, develop quickly while the wilted petals are still clinging to unpicked flowers. These unripe seeds look as if they would have a good flavor, pickled and spiced in vinegar. And in fact an herb book Joyce gave me does have an old recipe for pickling nasturtium seeds.

🌱 PEARL McCALL's large, faded-white house on her Daviess County farm seemed so expressive of her I was surprised to learn it did not become really hers until some years after she had moved into it, as Austin McCall's bride.

She has lived alone there since Austin's death. Sometimes some of her high-school- or college-aged grandchildren spend long summer vacations with her. Her son John has a farm only a short distance further along the road and farms both farms, but Pearl continues to take care of the house, the flowers, the vegetable garden, and a chickenhouseful of white chickens, because she enjoys it.

It was already a week late for planting sweet potatoes, she said, leading us across the back porch, but she was still hoping to find plants to put into the sweet-potato ridge she had built up across the "near" end of the big garden.

We went into a large, remodeled kitchen, across a dining room, and sat in the living room, where an assortment of chairs and a sofa were arranged to face the television so they could all watch when John's whole family came. Near the television set was a piano, which one of her granddaughters plays well. One of the granddaughters reached third place in the Miss Indiana contest one year.

The house was built in 1881, by a farmer who later became Pearl's father-in-law. He had started as a bachelor in a small house on eighty acres. At thirty-two he married a woman ten years younger. By hard work and good management he increased his farm acreage until finally it required the labor of several hired hands, and they all lived with him in the little house. By that time he decided he needed a bigger house for his wife and children and hired men, so he sent for a carpenter to come and design one. He liked the design so well he didn't ask the cost but just said, "Build it." His wife trusted his judgment so completely she made not one suggestion about the house, which is probably why it has only one closet, a small one under the dining-room stairway. By the end of a year the house was ready to move into and the farm had grown to 465 acres. Of the several children, only one, Austin, lived to maturity. He stayed at home to help his father on the farm and married Pearl, a pretty girl with long dark hair and blue eyes.

She had always admired the big house with its carriage house out in front (now replaced by a bed of gladioli and roses). But her mother warned her, "If you go to

66

live in that house, remember it belongs to Austin's mother. Go with that knowledge and you'll never have any trouble."

So Pearl went with that knowledge, lived happily in the house, and when Austin's widowed mother died she left the house and the original eighty acres to Pearl and the rest to Austin.

Pearl and Austin farmed in the horse-drawn era when farmers raised big poultry flocks and sold eggs and frying chickens. They worked enthusiastically helping to establish Farm Bureaus and home-economics clubs and county fairs. Their tendency to community service survives in their son John, who takes a responsible part in the soil-conservation management for his county.

Pearl and Austin exhibited livestock and poultry at county fairs that in those days were more agricultural than industrial, she said.

The big house never had fireplaces. It was built to be heated by stoves. When Pearl and Austin had prospered sufficiently they replaced the heating stoves with a furnace. She told me happily, "And when we did that Austin told me, 'Pearl, this is real livin'.' " She smiled.

❦ ONE OF THE ITEMS listed in Gene Williams's advertisement for the Kiser sale in Spencer was "old meal chest."

You have to read Gene's sale bills with skepticism because although he is an honest auctioneer and does not misrepresent, he takes more than usual delight in those nostalgics called "antiques." He collects old framed lithographs and hangs them, not for sale at any price, on the walls of his sale barn near his farmhouse. He can go into raptures describing old-fashioned farm breakfasts, or a set of harness with brass rings, a cupboard put together with wooden pins, or an ugly old heavy-legged table. He isn't nearly as old as these enthusiasms suggest.

Dick has happy memories of the meal chest his Aunt Belle had in her big, cozy, unmodern kitchen near "Jerdan" in Owen County, when he was a boy living in town and yearning to live on a farm. He had promised to buy me the first meal chest he could find.

Abby Kiser's meal chest, sitting in an unheated shed among a lot of "stuff," was made of poplar boards twenty inches wide, all in good condition, painted green. Inside were two bins, big enough for a hundred pounds of flour and a hundred of cornmeal. Abby's brother made her the chest for a wedding present, and equipped it with a rolling pin that fits into a niche inside one bin, and a smooth, removable mixing board that covers one bin and can be slid to give access to either one. When we lifted the lid of the chest ninety years of flour and cornmeal fragrance rose up to meet us.

Dick stayed out in the cold to buy the chest, but I went inside to interview Ada Kiser, widow of Abby Kiser's son Felix. She still lives on the farm she and Felix owned, but had come that day to help Kiser relatives with the sale and she knew the stories of all the items being sold.

"Hundreds of pies and loaves of bread and cornbread have come out of that old chest," she said. She was pleased when Dick came in and said he had got the chest on a twenty-six-dollar bid. For thirty dollars, later, John Cissna removed the hard green paint and gave it back the honey-and-butter color old poplar deserves.

"Felix was only fifteen months old when his mother

Abby died, and his sister had to take over the care of the family," Ada told us. In 1901, when she was born, her parents were living on a rented farm in Owen County. Her brothers and sisters went to a country school but her parents moved into town before Ada was old enough to go to school. When she became engaged to Felix her mother prophesied gloomily, "Ada, you won't like living in the country." But she did. "I loved everything about farm living . . . the work, the changing seasons, the crops, the care of livestock and our children, and visiting Felix's sister.

"I helped Felix with the farmwork, even shucking corn. We used to get up early and shuck three loads, then I got supper while he shucked another load and did the chores. We had our own farm most of the time, but there were a couple of years when Felix's father couldn't do for himself or take care of the farm, so we went and lived with him those years."

She still loves the farm. Her married daughter built a new house across the road from Ada's; the son-in-law does the farming. The grandchildren have pets and riding horses and ride a school bus into town to school.

AN AUCTION EXPRESSES the personality of the auctioneer as much as things being sold express the householder. At the Kiser sale were things people bid on as if from a long-pent-up yearning. The nostalgics called antiques are relics of an earlier time, not always very long-gone, but in these relics people sense a vanished leisurely good that may not really have been there in the original time of use, or may at least have been less than it is remembered in retrospect. Possibly one reason people value these nostalgics is that their modern way of living doesn't depend on them, or require the people to live in the restricted way that made those things useful.

Gene likes them all, for whatever reason, and is never at a loss for a good word to say for whatever he picks up to sell. If it's some hideous oddity nobody is likely to want he can say, "Now, people, here's something you don't often get a chance to bid on." Among the nostalgics at the Kiser sale were some temptations, such as a blue-and-white coverlet woven in Germany with the date 1848 woven into it, and in perfect condition because Abby Kiser had always kept it only on the guest bed. A custard-glass pitcher with matching glasses created lively bidding. The man who finally got it on a bid of a hundred and five dollars reached out for it and discovered his hands were trembling so violently he didn't dare take it.

Among the less tempting was a nondescript semi-new cupboard with glass doors. Gene approached it, obviously trying to think what to say. I had taken paper and pencil, hoping to get a column from the interview with Ada Kiser, so I was able to write down exactly what he did say and it was exactly this: "Now, people, this is one of the fastest coming to the front in a china cupboard that we have had." The cupboard brought twenty dollars and Gene's compliment was worth half that.

☙ SOME PEOPLE like old houses so much they can't bear to live in new ones. Two such couples are Garrett and Marie Berry, and their son Bill and his wife. They live in charming old houses in Coal City.

Strip mining was originally the bread and butter of Coal City. Its jam was provided by surrounding farms.

Shop buildings were narrow, deep rooms of soft old brick, trimmed with painted wood. It is an old town and its population has never exceeded a thousand. Many of its original houses are now dilapidated, but were sturdily built and had enough character to inspire a wish to restore and live in them.

When Garrett Berry retired from the Indianapolis police force, he and Marie wanted to live in a quiet country town, so they went back to Coal City, where as a child Marie had lived, with her grandmother. By that time somebody else owned "Grandma's" eighty-nine-year-old house, so the Berrys bought the old house across the street from it. Marie still has some of Grandma's furniture, including a little split-hickory rocker Grandma liked because she could sit on it and draw her feet up on it in front of her.

Marie said, "I just want you to see what Bill and his wife have done with four rooms." She took us across the back yard to the small, white-painted brick house. Bill's wife was washing Sunday-company dinner dishes. Housework and crewelwork are luxuries to her; on weekdays she works in nearby Terre Haute. Bill manages a squadron of vending machines, of which two were bivouacking in the living room that afternoon, waiting to be assigned to battle stations the next day.

We went into a large room that begins as a kitchen with hand-rubbed wood cabinets and a long row of old bottles and antique glass jars. Two steps farther it becomes the dining room with a long Early American table and tall ladderback chairs. From then on it becomes a living room, with a brick fireplace, and a floor laid of wide boards hand-scraped and made to shine. It is decorated with paintings and crewelwork by Bill's wife. "We learned all we know of carpentry from doing this house," Bill said. When they came to a complication too big for them they called in some Amish carpenters from nearby Daviess County.

They covered old ceilings with wide boards, put wood paneling on walls throughout the house, built louvered closets, hung a piece of crewelwork above the bathtub.

By this time they had discovered that if they could get into the attic, there was enough space there for another room. So they built a stairway rising from the big downstairs room and going up a short flight of steps to a square landing, enclosed by a railing. The landing has the fascinating character of a child's tree house. A child sitting on the landing could look down between railposts and see everything . . . kitchen, dining room with supper being put on the table, the fireplace, the television, the people, even the birds outside coming to eat from a bird feeder that hangs there among the evergreens pressing against the living room's bay window, giving a sense of wonderful privacy to a place that actually sits close to the street.

✢ "It's simple," said Brink Stillwater modestly when somebody complimented him on accomplishing an impossible job. "You just do what you can. There's lots of small detail in that. Then you do what you can't; there's less detail in that and it's harder."

The Heart Leaps Up

🐦 "Covet is a bad word," said Anita Frazier, taking me from field to field to look into bluebird boxes, "but I really coveted this twenty-three acres of wasteland joining our farm."

The bluebirds trust her. She can raise the lids of any of the sixteen boxes and even reach in to count the eggs or pick up the unfledged birds. "Until they are old enough to be afraid," she explained. She bands bluebirds for state records.

Her understanding of them and her passionate interest in the country environment are all the more remarkable because she grew up in a small Wisconsin town and never lived on a farm until she and Harris moved to Indiana.

She was graduated from the University of Wisconsin and went to Chicago "for a career," she says amusedly. She met Harris there and was attracted to him "because I thought he could teach me to ride horses." Harris had always lived in a suburb near Chicago except for ecstatic summers spent on a ranch in Colorado.

They married and lived in Chicago until their three children had grown and moved to distant places. Then Harris retired youngly and they "looked around for a piece of rough land we could buy cheaply and build up."

The two hundred acres they finally bought in Monroe County were totally "unimproved." Abandoned as farmland, it no longer had house, barn, or water supply. The Fraziers made a careful investigation of water getting, including water witching. They even corresponded with the author of a book about a renowned water diviner and then with the diviner himself, who is able to locate water veins even from a map. He told Anita their farm has nine water channels but he would have to come to Indiana to locate the exact spot. He lives in New England, so the Fraziers selected two sites and hired a local well driller to put down a well, unwitched, and they got water near the hilltop site they had first chosen.

Afterward, with advice from the Soil Conservation Service, they built a pond. The water is deep and clean enough to swim in. They put up a prefabricated house, a good barn, a great deal of fence, and swinging gates. They bought riding horses and purebred Hereford cows they called "The Girls." After a few years on the farm they gave up cattle and concentrated on race-horse breeding. They had a dog, a duck, and a spectacular variety of songbirds. They planted a big garden, a strawberry patch, rows of everbearing red-raspberries, trees, shrubs, and flowers. Their house has a fireplace and a dishwasher, this last, Anita explains carefully, "not because I wanted it, but it came with the house." Into the house they brought books, comfortable and pretty furniture, some of it made by Harris, who is skillful at his hobby of woodworking. He took part in community activities such as the county fair and the Soil and Water Conservation Service. Anita, who was popular in college and belonged to a social sorority and many campus organizations, does not care for social functions. She participates in book and art clubs and is perennially an officer of the Sassafras chapter of the Audubon Society.

In addition to the bluebird nests, she showed me nests of towhees, brown thrashers, cardinals, and chickadees. "I walk in the woods every day," she explained. She habitually wears old blue jeans, scuffed shoes, and a short haircut, without seeming sloppy or unfeminine, and has the gift of making you feel that everything you say is interesting.

She showed me a place in the woods where once, in daytime, she surprised a whippoorwill sitting on the ground. She knew where to look for winter ferns and the less common broad-leafed "sensitive" fern near a tiny stream of water.

It was evening as we walked toward the wasteland boundary. We were following a bridle path across the back pasture where clover was knee-deep. Anita rides there when none of her children or seven grandchildren is there to ride with her.

By the time the Fraziers had owned the two hundred acres for twelve years it had fattened like a calf grown glossy and plump from good feed and care. Then they bought the twenty-three acres of wasteland.

"This twenty-three acres," said Anita, in her pleasure practically singing the words, "had been corned to death before we got it. It was terribly eroded, and abandoned. Since it joins our land, I persuaded Harris we could run our horses on it when our pastures needed rest. At first he didn't want to buy it."

She wanted it because at heart she is an earth lover and wanted a more intimate relationship with the tulip poplars, maples, sassafrases, sumacs, and white oaks, and the bittersweet and dewberries on the ground, the blackberries rising square-stalked and thorny out of its woods, and the many birds that came to eat them. She wanted the splotches of reindeer moss and the gray-green lichens on the ground. She had familiarized herself with all of these. When I exclaimed about how much she knows she replied modestly, "Well, you know, when you're interested in something, you learn about it."

So we came to the wasteland and my heart leaped up.

A farmer's heart leaps up when he beholds a well-tilled, fertile field in any stage of production. If a non-farmer's heart leaps up at the sight of a field of ripe wheat or a cornfield sparkling greenly in sunlight, it is because in his subconscious ancient memory he associates it with his own food. A preservationist's heart leaps up at the sight of any kind of land . . . farm, wilderness, jungle, tundra, prairie, or swamp just lying there with no harvest being exacted of it. For true earth lovers the most heart-upleaping sight of all is the sight of abused land showing that it can heal itself and being given the opportunity to do it.

The fields on the twenty-three acres had been kept in corn until their strength gave out. To create those upland fields in the first place, the original farmer had cleared away trees and bushes. As the fertility was used up in the fragile, red-yellow sandstone soil and nothing was put back, the crop failed a little more each year. Each year more of the unprofitable field had been left untilled and in those places trees and bushes had begun to come back. By now trees growing in the abandoned field were ten to twenty years old. There was a great variety of them, and some were large. Finally bushes, weeds, and briers had retaken the open spaces entirely.

In the years when the fields were still being planted to corn, the soil had been left without a cover crop through winter and plowed again in spring. Without anything to hold the topsoil in place, the land was eroded cruelly.

It began with water running in little threads, never making real streams, but merely creating trickles that in every rain carried away a little more of the starved soil. Water came down the slopes and its runways branched out like the skeleton of a leaf, forking, cutting deeper as it ran, and running further after each rain. Eventually it had created room-deep, V-shaped tunnels. What remained of the field was cut up into long, narrow fingers of red-yellow ridge. It was so wasted that ordinary soil-conservation practices, terracing, sodded waterways, and watersheds were useless. Harris and Anita planted hundreds of evergreens, putting in one wherever it was possible to plant one.

But at the foot of the finger peninsulas nature, in her own way, had begun to heal the abandoned land. Birds and wind carried in seeds. Trees grew up, briers and bushes and vines crept over the stony places. Some few grasses and weeds that can endure harsh living came and took hold.

It was an eloquent statement of earth's resilience; a stern reminder that the land never really belongs to man; it is an arrogance and a costly mistake on his part to think so. It is his only to hold in trust, to use, and to share with his fellow citizens of earth, the wildlife and plant life by which nature keeps the balance of life.

When man destroys his relationship with these, he destroys his own security. When he finally abandons what he has destroyed nature will take it back and begin slowly, with infinite patience and skill, to restore it or create some new thing.

This is the heart-upleaping facet of the long view. And if, as the Interior Department's yearbook says, land is being carried away into the sea at the rate of 800 million tons a year, perhaps eventually the positions of land and sea will be reversed and nature will go right on creating.

It was a comforting thought on which to let an evening close. Anita and I walked back thoughtfully through the lush clover field.

"Goodbye," she said, having gone with us to open and shut the lane gate. Her voice sounded jubilant, like the singing voice of a little girl.

The Heart Leaps Up

🕊 NEXT TO INTERNATIONAL DIPLOMACY there's probably nothing more delicate than the silken case to which an Agalena spider entrusts her September eggs, and the tent-shaped, white-on-white covering she puts over it. This commonplace cocoon is remarkably waterproof.

Last fall I sometimes saw an Agalena running over the red cedar chunks that were to be cut into firewood and left outdoors to the battering of winter weather. The tree had died before the log was cut, making an air space between the bark and the fragrant wood and there the harsh crumbs of inner bark combined with the dry mycelium of spent fungus to make a rough, earthy walkway for spiders.

Agalenas like such places. This week when I pulled off some pieces of cedar bark I found three egg cocoons. The Agalena begins by making a round, flat, silken cushion as big across as a pencil's diameter. The eggs are laid on this, then over it, from many layers of thread so delicate it is invisible except by a microscope, the spider weaves a peaked tent. The layer starts against the inner bark, just at the edge of the cushion. Each successive layer begins a little further out until finally a waterproof density is achieved. Then at the peaked center of the tent all threads are gathered together into a cable no thicker than a piece of old-time grocery string. They hold together, without being tied into a knot, because they are slightly resinous. The cocoon thus has a yielding way of resisting dislodgement, or a resisting way of yielding, as you prefer. When I tried to pull the tent away from the bark it pulled apart into a confusion of delicate, clinging silken threads.

It is a commonplace thing, but remarkable. After be-

79

ing out all winter, with no maternal overseeing, the co-coon was still whole and waterproof. Agalena trusted her posterity to her silken threads and skillful weaving. For these spiders, having deposited their egg cases and covered them, do not live through winter. Immortality rests in the silken cushion.

🦅 As I WALKED down the rocky hillside back of Ira's barn to the woods creek that runs all year, I discovered plantain-leafed pussytoes velvetly in bloom. It was the first day of May, wet and slightly chilly.

Pussytoes grows in thin soil and can survive hot, dry weather. It was growing in a little island of thin soil set on a rocky slope from which, further down, a large bur oak has grown. From a short distance the flower of pussy-toes resembles the meager white flower of lady's-tobacco. A long stem rises from a rosette of elongated leaves that are always slightly whitened as if they had been dusted with flour. The plant grows only eight or nine inches high. Its flowerbuds, off-white, soft as a kitten's furred toes, and shaped like them, appear in a cluster of five on the tip of each center stalk. One cluster to a stalk.

The leaves remain when the flower is gone, and look like ordinary plantain leaves that just never had enough nourishment to grow big. I have seen rosettes of this flower in stony, yellow sandstone soil that had never known the taste of humus. In time of drought the plants are able to survive, holding the scanty soil in place, and usually in company with lichen-splotched stone slabs and thin layers of dry green moss. In spring it is sometimes companioned by scraggly little dandelions, in scorching midsummer by a few blades of wiry grass. For all of its velvety softness pussytoes is one of nature's tenacious soil holders and I respectfully avoided stepping on it as I went on down to the creek at the foot of the hill.

🪶 THE POND AT IRA'S is drying up in this time of drought. It never was very deep, being fed only by rain run-in. The drying outer edge gives a hint of how a drying lake might look; the soil reddish brown and cracked, porous as the end of an old bone and in places crusted over with a mineral salt, small black beetles swarming over the mud, and plants sprouting almost immediately behind the receding water. Last year Dick put small catfish into this pond; now they are eight to ten inches long, and as the water grows more shallow we see them jumping distressedly in the small peninsulas or resignedly lying still and their dorsal fins showing up as gray bumps above the pale water.

In the wet silt near the pond's edge, bony handprints show where a raccoon has walked, anticipating easy shore dinners of catfish. We decided to fish Ira's pond. Dick brought the diplander, which looks like a basketball net sewed shut on the lower end and fastened onto a long pole. He filled an old milk can with fresh water and set it into the truck bed so we could keep the fish alive until we got them to the big pond back of the barn where water is always plentiful.

It was easy to scoop up the big fish. They came up out of the shallow water, threshing and throwing mud around. Their mouths opened and their yellow undersides gleamed wetly in the late-afternoon sunlight. Dick said, "This is the kind of fishing I like. You don't have to bait a hook, or clean the fish afterward."

We took turns dragging the diplander through the water. We found a little painted turtle in the water, and on the bank of the pond I discovered a flowering weed called hound's-tongue. A great many plants of it grow further along the slope that goes down into the woods. Hound's-tongue grows two feet tall. Its narrow leaves taper gracefully to a point, and are rough on both sides, giving validity to its name.

The five-petaled flower is a poke-juice red. At that late point in its growing season the stalk held both flower and seed pod and looked unkempt, which is probably why the herbalist calls it gypsy plant.

The dime-sized seed pod is enclosed by five sepals and marked off into four parts with a single spike rising at the center. I pinched open one yellow-green, burry section of this fruitlet and saw the watery unripe seed inside. The brown stalk gave out an uninviting smell, sometimes compared to mouse smell. Old-time herbalists considered this plant valuable with reservations. Bee-keepers regard it kindly because it provides good honey material in the interim between fruit bloom and clover bloom. Sheepmen, however, can't say a single good word for it because the burry seeds catch in sheep's fleeces. I liked it because it is pretty and interesting and we were having a good time fishing when I first saw hound's-tongue.

🌿 THE BEHAVIOR OF EARTH, protecting some of its belongings under shelter of others, recklessly discarding some, and re-using some as the foundation of new projects, can be observed in unspectacular places, such as the raspberry patch where yesterday I cut weeds. Every summer there is relentless competition for every inch of this place. First the towering fountains of raspberry cane reach down to touch the ground, take root, and start a new plant. Unchecked they would soon become a thicket.

They have to compete with various societies of weed. Some weeds, such as Venus's looking glass, dayflower, and jimson, are pretty enough to be used in a flower garden if they were not so prone to overmultiply. The same objection applies to those that are edible . . . black mustard, pokeberry, curly dock, wild lettuce, all of which make delicious greens in spring. I have left catnip in the garden because I saw a goldfinch perched on its tall stalk and eating its seeds.

The wild vegetation grows in societies according to height. Under tall pokeberry, which birds love, and sweet rocket, which is pretty and fragrant but escapes all boundaries, and the other tall ones, the shorter plants subsist. Yesterday I met bull nettle, violets, Peruvian daisy, and many of their short friends under these tall sponsors.

Under all these, in the raspberry patch yesterday was a newcomer, swamp elder, which in its own mysterious way has crept up from the front corner of the yard. It is a jungly plant with an attractive, thin, serrated leaf and a stalk that looks like a pale-green glass tube filled with water. It has a tiny, inconspicuous white flower. It had chosen space under the short weeds, where there would always be shade and moisture. It was as easy to pull up this plant by the roots as to lift a wad of tissue paper from a packing box. With these three levels fully occupied it would seem that all of the garden's living space would be taken. But under the swamp elder were patches of moss. Thriving, half-inch strands of living green tinsel rose from its furry green.

Earth can support a great deal of life in small space, but must do it in earth's own way. This is observable in many places over the farm. The unused silo is one such place. A few years ago when Dick discontinued feeding silage, a layer of about four feet remained in the silo. It was still good, usable cattle feed.

Nothing went into the silo to disturb this coarsely chopped, pale-brown, pickled corn, except the earth-building agents of the natural world. Within a few years they produced what, to me, seems a small, lovely miracle. The silage became covered with short, richly green vegetation rising out of a layer of moist, black soil that smells like woods soil.

The first green was a liverwort, *Pellia epiphylla*. It may have started from a seed dropped by wind or bird into the roofless silo. It took root and increased by nature's thrifty way of filling up empty spaces. It has no real stalk; it is merely a coarse, hairy leaf the size of a breakfast cornflake set on edge. It can be lifted out easily and its roots, almost invisibly fine, glisten. By now most of the cornflake leaves have developed a tiny green cup at the center. The cups are somewhat like the green flowers on a stalk of bells-of-Ireland. Presently the beginnings of five-leafed ivy appeared in the silo and after a while the vine was climbing up three feet high against the acid-eaten, smooth inner wall of the concrete-block silo. Then little trees began to appear, sassafras, wild cherry, and hackberry.

To see that a green plant can thrive in the acid juice of the silage is surprising. Even more so is to see the newly made topsoil. It is black, loose, and has the pleasant smell of fresh woods earth or the morels one finds in the woods in April.

Only a few inches under this the silage is still pale yellow-green and could be fed to cattle. By now the top four inches has become a floating mass that can be gently moved back and forth with a pitchfork. It is, in exquisite miniature, an everglade swamp, and speaks cogently about the beginnings of earth.

🌢 THERE HAVE ALWAYS BEEN some plants of Solomon's-seal in the south bank near the mailbox. It does well in rich, neutral, limestone soil which the south bank offers, being in the heart of a well-known building-stone area.

After all the earth-scraping necessitated by repaving this road last summer I was afraid the Solomon's-seal would be gone, but this summer there is more of it than before.

In spring the plumes bend gracefully toward the road, three feet long and set with narrowly oval leaves that are heavily ribbed and grow in opposite rows. The greenish-white flowers, like deep little bells, hang in clusters from the plume's underside. By midsummer the flowers have given way to pea-sized green berries and by October the berries are dark blue, suspended from wiry, long stems and concealed under the leaves. Late in the fall the ribbed, taffeta-smooth leaves turn a luminous golden brown.

Looking at the berries you think they would spurt out a quick blue juice if you bit into one. Instead they contain a sedate, gelatinous green pulp with six or seven hard, pale-green seeds in each berry. I tasted the pulp and found it sweet, slightly brackish. Birds like these berries. They peck out the lime-colored pulp and the seeds, leaving the emptied hulls like bee-sucked grapes, hanging from the long stems.

Roots of this lily-related plant are knobby and scarred from stalks grown up out of them in earlier years. In Turkey these stalks are sometimes cooked and eaten like asparagus. Early American herbalists used the roots to treat bruises.

It must have been a scholar who named this plant, thinking the root scars resemble the ancient seal of King Solomon. This seal was made by a light triangle interlaid with a dark one so that all points show and it was believed to enable Solomon to predict the future. It may be the seal referred to in those poignant lines from the Biblical love poem . . . "Set me as a seal upon thine heart, as a seal upon thine arm."

Certainly this common roadside plant seems to be a literary personality, with its seal-like root scar, the pen suggestion of its plumy stalk, and the ink-blue berries hanging from it.

WHEN STARLINGS COME to the feeders other birds depart like leaves blown in the wind, to watch hiddenly and return only when the starlings have gone.

Hearing the high-pitched cacophonous chatter . . . for starlings always come by hundreds . . . I need only open the porch door and immediately they lunge forward, admirably regaining their balance when airborne.

The eight-inch bodies are darkly beautiful in metallic glints of purple, green-blue, and black with lines of

bright polka dots. They have short tails; their long, sharp
bills are brighter yellow in summer than in winter. They
strike greedily into mounds of suet in the feeders. Then
they wipe their bills sidewise, each side, against the rough
bark of the peach tree and you almost expect to hear them
belch.

Starlings like living near people because of the easy
food, but they grow restless when they feel they are
being watched. This spring they discovered Dick's un-
covered wagon of ground corn in the machinery shed.
Sparrows have known about it for years and have splashed
the faded red sides liberally. All the farm poultry know
about it and eat there freely.

Having found it, starlings came by thousands. They
threatened to become a major problem until one night
Dick covered the wagon with a tarpaulin and they never
returned to it again, though other birds did.

Farmers detest starlings and don't understand why
they were deliberately imported from Europe in 1890.
They do eat insects. I have seen starlings perch on the
backs and heads of the cattle here and pick off flies, while
the cattle stand placidly as if glad to be a part of the
symbiotic process.

Town people resent them just as bitterly and with
equal reason. Starlings roost on the courthouse window-
sills and around the dome, and people complain that they
are noisy and dirty. But on some nights when I have been
Christmas shopping late in the evening I have watched
the starlings flock in to their customary roosting places
at dusk, and it was rather pleasant to watch. They come
crying and calling, and the sound is poignant.

But these dark-bodied birds awaken a dark thought
in the mind of a farmer: It is not merely because they eat

food not intended for them, nor because they are dirty, but because there are always too many of them. Any creature that becomes too numerous causes unease among all other creatures.

Cardinals are welcomed because of their brilliant plumage and their sweet songs. They have some ugly monotonous words, too, and the males are often abusive to the females. Would cardinals be as welcome if they came in droves, as starlings do? Or would ten thousand gaily singing chickadees be as delightful on a snowy winter morning as half a dozen are?

The old adage "There's safety in numbers" has a reverse side; there's danger in numbers, too. *National Wildlife* magazine said in March 1969, "The ultimate reason for destruction of wilderness, for air pollution and the extinction of wildlife is simply too many people." The editor told me, "There have been scores of letters voicing this thought."

🕊 A GRACKLE CAME to the feeder this morning and stood solemnly on the roof, sidewise, so one pale, fierce eye could better watch the porch window from whence cometh no help to him, as a rule. For several seconds while he stood as if contemplating a bitter truth, I had a fine opportunity to observe him. He has elements of genuine beauty. When he turned his flat, dark, sleek head downward, its colors changed from black to marvelous blue. The eye is too pale, the long bill too suggestive of cruelty. But he stood alone and he looked as fiercely patriarchal as the ancient Biblical prophets, as savage as a primitive tribal chief.

I thought about how different the world would be if all the birds were large and able to defend themselves.

This year grackles came to the farm in hordes, and stayed. Shooting seemed not to discourage them or diminish their numbers.

At a supper one evening the subject of grackles came up and voices around the table gave a collective denunciation: "They're so destructive; they ruin a place wherever they stay." "They're so dirty." "They drive out other birds and there are more of them every year." "You have to kill the first ones and before the trees leaf out or they'll take over completely." "They're intelligent; they know just how far beyond gunshot is safe." Dick said, "They're first out in the morning, last going in at night, watching to see where the other birds are nesting so they can destroy the nests."

Then a man who used to be a farm boy and keeps his feeders filled for songbirds the year round said, "It may be there are lots of grackles because grackles have been able to survive what the more-loved songbirds could not."

To smaller birds, the arrival of grackles may be somewhat as it was for prehistoric animals when man arrived on earth and began to multiply and dominate.

One thing humankind must admire about these fierce invaders: grackles can get along with other grackles.

ꙮ THE CHIEF BUSINESS of this farm is beef production, and however the steers may differ from year to year, they have two invariable basic traits: avid curiosity and the ability to find the easiest level for climbing up a hill.

One year they began to explore the joys of the creek valley back of Ira's barn. Later they explored the first hillside. There the creek runs between what we call the Near Hill, the Middle Hill, and the Far Hill. All hills tempted the cattle. They began climbing up into the hill woods, and finally this became intolerable to me.

There is no gain in pasturing a wood. There is nothing in it for cattle to eat, and the fragile, fragrant woods loam cannot withstand the pathmaking of their sharp, cloven hoofs.

In the wilderness of these hills are rock ledges big enough to sit on with a portable typewriter beside you, and underneath are the scooped-out entrances to dens of woods animals. There are spicewood, papaws, wild cherry, red haw, wahoo, redbud, dogwood, sassafras, green brier, wild grape. There are tall straight tulip poplars, walnuts, hard maples, hackberries, hickories, white oaks and bur oaks, honey locusts and pignuts and sycamores. There are ferns, wildflowers, weeds, and grasses. There are different kinds of stones, and geodes beautiful and ancient, in the hillsides. Wilderness is a perishable treasure. When it's gone, it's gone forever, but steers are replaced every year.

So I told Dick, "I will help you fence the wilderness. This week." He went to the Farm Bureau and came home with steel fence posts and spools of barbed wire.

It took three days of intensive work to put up the fence. Only a person who loves wilderness could work so tenaciously, carrying spools of barbed wire into places where you couldn't go with the unspooler, a handy home-made thing contrived from the wheels and handles of an old-fashioned push lawnmower, and driving steel posts with a wooden maul into the stony hillside. Dick plotted a fence contour with a minimum of brace-demanding angles. We hauled posts, fence stretchers, sledge hammer, boxes of fence-staples, which farmers call "steeples," and hand tools on the flat-bed tractor wagon as far as possible and carried them the rest of the way. On steep wooded hillsides we walked backward, carrying barbed wire and trusting not to slide downhill onto the rocks in the creek. Also rapturously taking note of woodpecker nests in hollow, dead trees, and new patches of fern, and fossil-filled stone slabs. It takes less breath to think than to talk, so in fencing one doesn't talk much. Thinking, I revised Omar Khayyám's wilderness rhapsody:

> A roll of barbed wire carried 'neath the bough,
> Sledge hammer, "steeples," metal posts, and thou
> Beside me, fencing in the wilderness.
> Ah, wilderness will soon be safe from cow!

Cattle have to come down to drink from the "riffle" in the creek, Dick insisted, because the water never goes dry there and never freezes, so we had to leave access to it. We stretched barbed wire across the creek, and to prevent steers going under the wire, we dangled pieces of stone-weighted wire from the cross-wires. At the creek's edge, the stones were varied and fascinating, and while I selected the ones to dangle from the wires, I had a yearning to stay and gather up piles of stone. This, I am sure, is an ancient human instinct and may have been how stone houses began.

The cattle watched the fence building with great interest, benignly. After three days of this creation we rested, physically and spiritually.

That July, taking a class of city children on a tour of the wilderness, I fell on the creek's stone bed and broke my writing arm. It was the same place where several years ago Uncle Bent Stanger fell and broke a leg and his nephew carried him up out of the woods. Last year one of Dick's best young cows fell at the same place and broke her leg. Uncle Bent and I fared better than she did; we didn't have to be slaughtered.

Nevertheless, I love the wilderness.

🐦 AS THE CITY SPREADS OUT and in its light-making moves closer to this farm, the wild places seem every year smaller and more vital. There are plants growing on the Middle Hill that I have never seen elsewhere; some, numerous in pioneer times, are scarce now. Yesterday I saw camas, a small hyacinth hunted by Indians in spring because they liked its oniony flavor. The pale lavender flowers had already bloomed. There also I found golden ragwort, which is interesting because it has two kinds of leaf, a round one growing at the base, a long narrow one higher up on the stalk. The flower is a richly yellow daisy shape, blooming in a cluster at the end of the stalk.

This spring on the Middle Hill we found big morel mushrooms, and while looking for mushrooms I found two flowers new to me, and I felt like William Bartram exploring America in the seventeenth century. Golden seal and horse gentian were both more plentiful in William Bartram's day than now.

Golden seal bears only one flower to a plant. The stalk rises between sharply serrated, red-green leaves the color of new blackberry leaves. The center becomes a a seed fruit resembling a deep red raspberry. Horse gentian, also called feverwort, has a broad, imperturbable-looking leaf similar to the leaf of ironweed. Dark-red tubelike flowers with large green pistils rise where the leaves rise, and are surrounded by red, leaflike projections that resemble flowers. These later enclose an orange-red fruit, which early New Englanders sometimes roasted and used for coffee.

↯ TWO THINGS ALWAYS impress me when I go to the wilderness: One is how I always discover something new there; the other is how glad I am there is still some wilderness to go to.

Time was in America when people went to an untouched spot in a forest or beside a clear river, or into a desert or up a mountainside or onto a wide, grass-covered prairie, and took along what they poetically called "a dream," which was the hope of building a home there, or a city, or a society. Too often that dream came true.

Now finding some untouched spot one has a different, equally passionate dream . . . the hope of leaving it alone, letting it stay exactly as it is except for the changes time and nature make, in the continuation of evolution. This is a luxurious dream, and always subject to new menace by people who have the first kind of dream.

I went to the woods yesterday, not so much in the hope of escaping my problems as to rest my mind so I could endure and later try to solve the problems.

It is not only plants that make the wilderness a rest to the spirit. Living creatures also have a claim; the yellow butterflies I saw hovering restlessly over a mudhole, the solitary monarch flitting through the woods, the rabbit sitting thoughtfully in the middle of a bare spot of earth. Finally to my astonishment I saw a red fox. I was walking down the hillside. He was sitting on a big clean stone, eating something, and did not see nor hear me.

93

His back was turned to me and I watched while he chewed. When he had finished, he still had not seen me, but loped away, deeper into the wilderness. I looked at his stone but could not find any crumb to show what he had been eating.

✠ GUIDED BY JUNE FULFORD, who remembers Honey Creek when its country schools were still in use, we drove through an area that has lately received considerable publicity.

At one time the community had a church, two one-room township schools, the Farr and the Honey Creek, a country store, and several self-sustaining small farms.

The store has been gone a long time. Only a small cleared space, between a thicket and the edge of the road, shows where it was. The road forks there, one fork going on to the old siding-covered log house where the original grocery owner lived. The other fork leads on up between evergreen-studded hills to where, between 1933 and 1942, a Civilian Conservation Corps camp was based. Only traces of the camp remain now, including the scornful name by which it was known in the community.

But the church is still in use, small, white, lovingly kept. Gravestones come up close all around it. Near the front is a life-sized statue of a soldier in the doughboy uniform of World War I. It honors young Forest Riddle, who came home safely from that war and died of flu in his father's house. His youngest brother died the day before from the same illness. Nobody told him, but Forest guessed it and asked. There were several sons and daughters in the family. Their father was a leader in the community, loved and trusted. His family lived in a big, hos-

pitable white house on a hill within walking distance of
the church and he was a pillar of the church. On Sunday
there were always many guests at his house for dinner. In
preparation, Mrs. Riddle and her daughters filled the "pie
safe" with fresh pies.

The children and grandchildren moved away into
other communities, where many of them became leaders.

In the days when Honey Creek's schools were in use,
pupils walked to them, carrying lunches. It was seldom
more than two miles from any home to the school, and
pupils sometimes carried books, but in that agricultural
community "homework" was farm chores, not school as-
signments.

The farms changed hands. New families came in
and left. New houses have been built, mobile homes and
abandoned cars have appeared. The people are no longer
agricultural. Most have jobs in nearby towns. Part of the
area has recently been looked on covetously, by a city in
search of a landfill garbage disposal.

At one place along the road June said, "This area is
in the Community Action Program." In some places
houses clustered wretchedly amid trash; dogs ran out and
barked at the car. But there were places where magnificent views of woods and hill and curving road inspire one
to cry out reverently, "For heaven's sake, let us preserve
the countryside and keep it clean!"

🌿 "As I understand it," said Brink Stillwater,
farmer, whose wife does the family's blackberry picking,
"the worst thing about berry pickin' is not the chiggers
nor the sweat nor the briers, but your brassiere strap
suddenly breakin'."

95

Paper Making Is an Old Art

❦ DURING THE SUMMER when leaves concealed their
coming and going, a society of hornets built a nest in a
young maple just outside the stone fence enclosing the
Maple Grove church. Although the tree is barely twenty
steps from the front door, few worshippers saw it and nobody got stung.

Autumn's leaf fall revealed this gray paper artwork

and I wanted it. It would be empty by then, I knew, because hornets do not live through winter, except the large, fall-impregnated queen, whose business it is to survive in a safe place and start a new colony the next spring. Also I knew that if it were left in the tree, the empty nest would be quickly torn to shreds by birds seeking dead hornets to eat. Already a couple of loosened strips fluttered like gray petals in the November wind.

"The church would be glad to give it to you," said the church treasurer, my neighbor Clyde Naylor. But in behalf of the tenant hornets I paid him five dollars for rent of church property, and Dick persuaded Carr to help us saw the nest limb out of the tree. They handed it down undamaged and at closer view it was even more admirable, about the size and shape of a steer's head, made of horizontal layers of rumpled, heavy paper marked in parallel striations of brown on shades of gray. Through the hornets' entrance at the lower, tapered end, we could see tiers of white-tipped cells, empty now, the sealed-in eggs having been hatched, fed, and assigned to different tasks in the summer society and all done now. This entrance had already been slightly enlarged by hungry birds, probably tufted titmice, which specialize in this kind of demolition.

All summer, as the queen laid more eggs in more cells, the working caste had gone into the nearby woods and chewed up more old wood into a paste which they carried back to the nest, working it down into a strip of gray paper and biting it into place against already existing layers. With something of humility I held the nest on my lap as Dick drove home down the hill.

In the house, when I shook the nest lightly a few sluggish hornets and one large queen fell out. All their faces were marked with white. I put the workers into a glass jar, where some remained dead, but a few revived enough to climb restlessly up the side of the jar, stepping unconcernedly over the dead bodies of their comrades and steadily making the droning noise of a small motor. I put the queen outside, hoping she would find safe winter quarters quickly.

Dick put a couple of hooks in the porch ceiling so that the nest suspended from them would hang exactly at the same angle as in the tree. Unfortunately the warmth of the enclosed porch revived the late-summer odor of the nest. Hornets do not store up honey, but they do bring food, preferably caterpillars, into the nest. Their mouths are too small to eat solid food, so they suck out the juices, then work the rest into little pellets which they carry home. By late summer their housekeeping is careless. They leave the garbage around and the smell of it some-times entices flies to come in and lay eggs there. The nest acquires a cloying body odor, unpleasant at close range. We hung the nest in a shed, protected in a plastic sack, until the smell had faded. By that time all the dead hor-nets had fallen out, too.

Putting the queen outside I was startled to notice the similarity between the shape of her head and the shape of the tapering nest. It could be mere coincidence, of course, or the logical outcome of some building principle used by hornets. But considering that the paper makers have no previous experience and no blueprints to go by, and yet make all nests over a similar pattern, it may be they model their architecture over the first and greatest object of authority they know.

The renowned modern sculptor Henry Moore has said, "Every shape, every little bit of natural object has

99

meaning if you can just find it." Actually, whether you
find or merely look for the meaning, it has meaning. Perhaps the gray paper nest, shaped like a queen's head, is a
hymenopterous Taj Mahal, perhaps even a way of hornet
worship.

Wasps and hornets knew how to make paper long
before the Egyptians made it from their papyrus reed or
the Chinese made it from the inner bark of mulberry trees
mixed with other fibers. Yet every new hornet society
has to begin totally without previous experience. From
the standpoint of reverence inspired by this fact, the
church tree was an appropriate choice of site for the
hornets. The queen building the first hurried nest in the
spring, in which to lay eggs and hatch a batch of hornets
for workers, builds only the flattish, celled, inner layer.
When the workers mature they cover it with the gray
paper.

Perhaps one reason I admire hornets is that I have a
respect for paper and it is important to me. I enjoy the
immaculate look of fresh white bond in undisturbed
reams, or the sight of new notebooks, or boxes of station-
ery. But I cannot do creative or even comfortable writing
on such paper. It intimidates me. My thoughts seem un-
worthy and recoil before its nobleness.

I sympathize with hornets that choose old, weathered logs and dead leaves and old boards for their paper-
work. Probably they find it easier to chew up and more
readily blendable with their paste-making mouth juices.

My writing is the same. My thoughts flow more
easily on unimposing paper, especially paper that has
already been used on one side and would otherwise be
thrown away. I like to write on the backs of old form

letters, or advertising bills torn into pages. I can express myself more accurately and with less inhibition on such paper.

When a manuscript is polished to the last comma and therefore requires no further cross-examination, I can copy it on fresh sheets of that yellow manila paper called "second sheets" but never on crisp white bond. I used up the whole yellow manuscript of my first book to write first drafts of newspaper columns long before Boston University's Mr. Gotlieb asked me for my papers. It lasted a long time and I wrote many unhampered columns on it.

There may be a reasonable explanation for this. It is probably not so much from thrift or modesty as from an awareness that paper is made from trees, and I cannot bear to waste natural resources. I cannot burn weeds or leaves that can go into the garden as a mulch, either, although I love to sit by a wood-burning stove or fireplace, to see the flames and smell the fragrance. For the Franklin stove in the kitchen I gather up old boards and poles and fallen maple limbs as much as possible, because this seems like giving the waste wood a new usefulness, in fact a kind of immortality.

It is the same with paper that has been used on one side. To write something worth writing on paper that has already served once seems good. When the farm's son and daughter went out into their separate working worlds, leaving me a heritage of old college papers and notebooks to write columns on, it seemed a richness.

This respect for paper may be a family trait. My sister Miriam Mason, who wrote children's books, was once asked by her publisher to send them a book manuscript quickly. All she had was a first draft written on the insides of used envelopes. She had no time to copy it and probably wouldn't have anyway, so she sent it. The publishers accepted it gladly and so did the children when it came out between hard covers, with illustrations.

On the other hand, I once had an uncle, a handsome and overly religious man who regularly steamed open the envelopes in which letters came to him. He refolded them with the clean side out and mailed out his own letters in them. He was never a rich man, but I think it was not poverty that inspired the use of old envelopes as much as it was a kind of religious self-abasement, the idea of making himself humble. He enjoyed doing this, I think, just as he enjoyed carpenter work at which he was a total failure. I think he liked the martyrdom of using poor envelopes to write to his friends and "do them a Christian service" by predicting when the end of the world would come and how few would survive.

In his ordinary letters to me he always quoted liberally from religious publications and told me about the coming doom and other such things. These letters were never very interesting to me. But when he answered my questions about Grandmother and how she cooked, and the time the milk cows were killed on the railroad tracks because the family had no fence on their little Minnesota homestead farm, and how his brother Vincent did the butchering while their father was away from home and later sold the beef . . . eighty-eight pounds at five cents a pound in 1887 . . . and the recipe by which Grandmother made "the best cookies I have ever baked," or how she cleaned and scoured the little Minnesota home and put clean "window papers" in the upstairs windows before she left the house forever to move back to Indiana

. . . these letters I thoroughly enjoyed. They gave life and validity to the re-used envelopes and made me want to be a better person, like Grandmother.

🐦 MY SISTER GRACE, the music teacher, making some small changes in her house, offered me a door and I accepted it. In the truck as we drove to her house, Dick asked me, "What are you going to do with this door?"

Probably nothing, except just keep it. I have a respect for doors. If you have an old, attractive, handmade door, you can always hope to get a house to fasten on to it.

There are other uses, too. A door is something to open wide when a friend comes; something to close against cold, or emptiness, or grudges. It is something to slam in anger, relieving your spirit, or hang a Christmas wreath from, or close in exquisite gentleness in time of sorrow.

A door is symbolical of something within yourself that you can close to avoid wounding a friend or being wounded by one; or when you are unwilling to strike back in angry justice, thus setting a stone between yourself and your friend that both of you will have to step over for the rest of your lives.

There are times when nothing in the world is as profoundly satisfying as simply to close a door.

🐦 SATURDAY WAS a perfect day for plowing; mild, sunny, the ground well settled. In this farming area all day, tractors sliced and turned the wintered gray surface of the cornfields.

Now in the evening there was a suggestion of rain

to come. Before supper we walked down to admire the cornfield Dick and a young town-dwelling friend had plowed that day.

The field lay stretched out around us, dark, promising, loamy brown. In the east it rose up slightly into a little knoll of the kind artists love to put into their pictures. There the soil was slightly more red and clayful than the rest and had therefore received extra loads of barnyard manure.

"This is the best job of plowing I have ever known this field to have," Dick said. I picked up a handful of soil, squeezed it into a ball, smelled it, crumbled it, and let it fall back onto the field. "What made the difference?"

"For one thing the plow was set just right . . . it's an awful good plow. And partly the speed and evenness of Jim's driving." A red-winged blackbird flew across the east corner as if late getting to his nest.

"You don't see a single furrow," Dick continued when we had finished watching the bird. "One round just overlaps the other exactly." The continuous, ruffled surface was an invitation to take off shoes and run barefooted across it.

"And you don't see a single cornstalk," he added. True, all the stalks of last year's corn were gone, as if they had not lain there all winter guarding the topsoil.

"It feels nice and mellow," I said, picking up another handful.

"Six hundred pounds of fertilizer to the acre, broadcast from a truck," Dick said, "and there'll be another hundred to go in with the planter."

A farmer is glad when the breaking is done, but enjoys seeing the brown furrows open up moist and fresh, and fall over just right, crumbling. To Jim the day's work had probably been spiritual refreshment. He had come in the morning intending to hunt mushrooms. When he learned Dick was breaking the cornfield he forgot about mushrooms and took over the plowing. Just as well; at that point of spring there were no mushrooms.

Late that night the mushroom rain began. In the freshly plowed field clods softened and grew companionable.

"This is the kind of rain I just love," Dick murmured late at night, "slow, soaking-in, gentle. You can just lie there and listen and know everything's all right."

↘ IN SEPTEMBER, Dick decided to have rye seeded by plane in eleven acres of standing corn.

This community is right in the path of planes coming into or leaving Allegheny's airport, and therefore the farmers are accustomed to the scream and thunder of jets, or military planes flying in formation and helicopters flapping not too far overhead. People pay little attention. Only the farm poultry take it excitedly. When jets are thunderous peacocks and guineas scream angrily and Bantams run for cover.

But when a small green-and-yellow biplane flew, low and circling Maple Grove fields, and came down in the alfalfa fields, that was different. It brought neighbors out of their houses in throbbing curiosity.

The pilot, Lewis Viech, came up from Vincennes in the late, rain-threatening afternoon. He is not permitted to fly directly above houses, so he circled around them and meantime a little audience was gathering in the alfalfa field. This kind of flying, because it has to be at low altitude and the plane could collide with power lines, is considered hazardous. Mr. Viech has, in fact, had some unplanned landings.

The biplane came down accurately in the alfalfa field where Dick had set up red flags and parked the truck with twenty-two bushels of seed rye in bright-green paper sacks. Balbo, $2.25 a bushel. By the time half of the seed was loaded into the grain hopper just in front of the tiny cockpit, an audience was watching. Carr, being nearest, arrived first and helped rip open the rye sacks. "Iris had supper about ready but I told her supper was going to be kinda delayed," he said. Knowing Carr's fear of heights, the audience jokingly urged him to hitch a ride on the yellow wing of the biplane.

Kevin, a young man on his way home from his job in town, said, "I've flown, but I wouldn't be comfortable flying that close to the ground." There was no room for a passenger, anyway. The plane can carry twenty bushels of seed at a load.

"I thought he was in trouble!" exclaimed neighborly Johnny Wilson, arriving from his Crossroads house.

"I'd seen your red flags, Dick, and knew what was comin' off," said Russell Fyffe, arriving in his truck and bringing the two young Peterson boys. "I was just gettin' ready to mow, but the mowin' can wait. I want to watch this."

The plane, tiny brother of the giant 747, is the kind used to train pilots in World War II, said Mr. Viech, who learned flying in military service in 1942.

That afternoon he had already sowed other farms in this county and last week sprayed five thousand acres of blight-struck corn in Daviess County. We watched the plane taxi out across the mowed alfalfa field, moving like a big farm wagon. Airborne, it turned at the end of the field, one wing pointing straight down, the other straight up, circled, and came back. We could see the grain flying out in a dark stream like smoke. After loading and sowing the second half Mr. Viech came past us, waved, and was on his way into the next county.

His total time, with temperature eighty degrees and wind variable, was forty minutes at $1.25 an acre plus one cent per pound. In all, $2.37 an acre, Dick estimated.

"It's worth that much just to watch the show," commented Russell.

"Beats sowing it with a one-horse drill," said Dick, as the cars and trucks pulled out to go home.

⟆ ALBERT HOLMES, born in Owen County on his grandfather's farm in 1881, says farming then was "a primitive, hard life, but interesting." He remembers it vividly.

"I dropped corn by hand and my brother Clarence covered it with a straddler. On Great-grandfather's farm near Gosport he had a flax hackle, candle molds, a reap hook, which is a kind of sickle for cutting wheat. He used a grain cradle with a two-tined fork for the wheat and had a wooden rake to use after mowing the wheat with a scythe. On that farm too were the tools for making the family's shoes. Grandfather used a mower-reaper and wooden-beamed plows, wooden plows to lay off rows, and a wooden A-harrow.

"When I tell my grandchildren about our tools and ways, how we tanned groundhog skins and cut shoe-laces out of them, they just grin. I tell them about the squirrel rifle, bullet mold, ramrod, the powder horn made out of a bull's horn; or I tell them about Grandmother's cord bed fastened together by ropes, her corner cupboards, the wooden bowls and churns for butter and cheese. I tell them of the things we gathered out of the woods, bluebells, buttercups, lamb's-tongue, horehound, catnip, and calamus.

"We used the knot maul, wooden gluts of dogwood, the hardest wood we knew, and wedges to split our wood with. We used a broadax and grubbing hoe.

"My grandchildren cannot imagine hauling haystacks with a grapevine for a chain, or stacking hay out in the field. But I remember the thrill of the threshing machine, threshing our grain, and I remember the ox team, Tim and Jerry, that hauled the Ashers' threshing machine from farm to farm."

Mr. Holmes also remembers the sudden sight of blacksnakes, the spotted water snakes, and "the thrill of finding an old groundhog in our favorite mulberry tree, and seeing the possum 'sull,' as we called it when he fell over and played dead. We could pick him up and carry him away by the tail when he was playing dead.

"My grandchildren can't believe any of it. Yet they know I am a truthful man if I am old."

Old-time farm memories, mentioned in letters to my farm column, seem mostly happy ones.

One morning Mr. Holmes seized a hungry pencil and wrote me about old-time orchards: "I am thinking about the old apples in the orchards, the horseapple, the sheep-nosed apple, the Vandiver, the Russet or Rustycoat, the Jackson, the Red Milan, the Grinstone and the Frostapple. The fall apples, the Limbertwigs, besides four different kinds of sweet apple.

"We had pears, too, on Grandfather Asher's farm; Clapp's Favorite, Duchesse d'Angoulême, and Noname.

There are people who have never tasted a ripe Mayapple or a red haw, or a black haw, and don't know how good papaws are."

Having got started on the thought of old-time foods, he was unable to stop. "And I think of sausage seasoned with red pepper, sage, and salt. I remember old-time liver-wurst, head cheese, and souse meat. And homemade mincemeat. My mother dried apples and made fried pies of them. I remember her apple dumplings boiled in a pot and warm with sweetened sour cream and a dash of nut-meg. Oh, and bowls of raspberry dumplings with top milk or cream!"

If he lives to be as old as a bristlecone pine, Mr. Holmes will probably still remember these things with pleasure.

A FEW MILES from here a long-time farm was about to go into a housing development. House and barns were going to be bulldozed away and the owner, a non-farming descendant of the original farmer, was going to give the obsolete machinery to his friends who would come and take it away.

Among the nostalgics surviving from an era before rural electricity, power farming, and the "cutout" system of government compensation, were such treasures as a side saddle, bridles, brass-knobbed hames, a tool chest, a fanning mill. There was also an old horse-pulled grain binder there.

Lex Hardisty said, "Dick, I really want the bull wheel off of that old binder." The owner had said he could have it if he would come and take it off.

Lex is not a farmer; he has a job at Crane Naval

Depot, but in his boyhood he lived on a farm and worked at others at various times. He lives in Ellettsville, a little Monroe County town, and drives eighty miles a day to his job. His married daughter lives on a little place in the Maple Grove community with her husband and two sons. Lex assuages his farm yearnings by helping them tend a garden and a large strawberry patch and by picking up persimmons from under the trees in their yard. The persimmons are large and tasty and never puckery, although they ripen long before frost. Every autumn Lex sets up an old-fashioned, hand-turned cider mill and makes gallons of cider.

He has a gift of good humor. When he isn't laughing or smiling he looks as if he were about to. When someone else is talking he listens, waiting to break into a smile, and he reminds me of a dolphin, which is known to be a creature of exceptional intelligence and good nature. Lex has had his share of genuine sorrow, but probably no experience has been so grim he couldn't afterward extract one good laugh from it, or at least one dolphinlike smile.

He was happily excited at the prospect of getting the bull wheel, but knew he would need help with it.

A bull wheel is a heavy, pressed-steel wheel with a double row of spokes and a cleated eight-inch rim. It was not for transporting the binder, but for supplying power to the moving parts. As the horses pulled the binder forward on transportation wheels, the bull wheel turned, thus powering the cutting knives that mowed barley, oats, rye, wheat, or any grain that was to be bound. It also turned the canvases that caught the mowed grain in bundles. The bundles were automatically kicked off, eight at a time, from the binder. They had to be picked up by hand and stacked in rain-shedding shocks in the field to wait until threshing day.

An old-time grainfield with the shocks set up at regular intervals all over it had a Biblical look, suggesting comfort and abundance.

On threshing day the shocks were hauled to the heavy, steam-powered threshing machine. The grain poured out in a brown stream from one spout. From another spout the clean, bright straw was blown, as if in its own private hurricane, into a great stack.

After threshing day was over and the big dinner accomplished, farm women emptied the old worn-out straw out of their mattresses called "straw ticks" and refilled them with fresh straw.

Inherently, therefore, the bull wheel which made all this possible was a symbol of power, expressive of the independent horse-drawn farming era. It was a more subtle symbol than the steam engine's piercingly shrill whistle which now brings nostalgic smiles to men who participated in old-time threshing days.

The removal of the bull wheel from the old binder was not going to be a one-man project, as Lex realized. So he invited help from fellow townsman Hugh Staudt, who once moved a house half a block to make himself a new home; and from his Maple Grove farming friend Dick, who had a pickup truck, wrenches, and as deep an appreciation of old-time machinery as Lex had.

The three friends spent a happy afternoon of hard work removing the wheel. By the time they had it off, evening was at hand. It was time for them to hurry home and do their chores and go to a Brotherhood supper at a country church. They loaded the wheel into the pickup and Lex said, "Take it home for tonight, Dick. I'll help

SPEAK TO THE EARTH

you unload it in my yard first thing in the morning."
Lex's town house is big, and surrounded by a big yard,
with trees in it.

Some of the Brotherhood wives always bring food
and help serve the suppers. Mary Hardisty brought her
peach-and-graham-cracker pudding and when she served
Dick she bent down and murmured, "Everybody needs a
bull wheel, Dick."

Early the next morning, before Dick had finished his
barn chores, Lex arrived. "I want you to have the bull
wheel, Dick," he said solemnly.

Then followed the usual exchange of declining and
thanks and re-offering and avowals of personal affection.
Finally Dick, who in research asks questions like a person going after a splinter in the thumb, asked, "Lex, is
this just from pure generosity, or because Mary won't
let you unload the bull wheel in your yard?"

After a couple of solemn seconds, Lex broke into his
engaging dolphin smile and admitted, "I'd rather not
say." Both men laughed heartily.

Now the bull wheel leans against a young maple just
outside of Dick's workshop. It still is a symbol of authority but nobody says whose.

In INDIANA's agricultural youth sorghum was one
of the farm staples, along with cured pork, lard, dried
apples and canned tomatoes, blackberry jelly boiled for
hours into a thin taffy, hulled walnuts, and sauerkraut.

Verna Greenlee, who has lived on a farm most of
her ninety-three years, remembers the pioneer ways with
blueprint accuracy. "When I was a child on my father's
farm seven and a half miles north of Greenfield, he al-

ways said just before frost, 'Time to get the sorghum ready to cut.' "

The cane patch, Verna explained, was in the cornfield because her father thought the flavor of sorghum was determined by the kind of soil it grows in. He preferred a spot of well-drained clay, the same as for corn. The children dropped and covered the small round seeds in spring. Later they thinned the plants to three or four in a hill. The cane was plowed when the corn was plowed. Before frost the blades were stripped off and put aside to be fed to cattle. Then Verna's father cut off the grain heads to feed later to the poultry.

Finally the bare stalks were put through a press that extracted the juice. Next the juice was boiled down, skimmed as it boiled, and finally run off into clean containers. The oldest cane mills were pole mills, turned by a mule or horse hitched to a long pole and walking in a circle.

"When I married in 1898," said Verna, "I lived near Coatsville in Hendricks County. My husband's family raised sorghum cane and had their sorghum made at the factory in Putnam County, near Fillmore. Sorghum was delicious on biscuits or pancakes or in gingerbread, but you could boil it forever and it wouldn't boil down into candy.

"I've seen my mother add it to beans she was baking. And we had a cookie recipe we liked. Take a cup of sugar, one of sorghum, half a teaspoon of ginger if you like it, a teaspoon of soda, a cup of shortening, and enough flour to make a very stiff dough. The cookies were hard when they first came out of the oven, but kept in a stone jar they softened after a few days.

" 'Slow as sorghum molasses' is awfully slow. In

winter I was often sent out to draw a crock of sorghum from the barrel in zero weather. It was a big barrel, laid across two chunks of wood, and had a faucet in the head. Oh, how long it took to fill that old brown milk crock! And I knew I didn't dare set it down and go off and leave it."

Today's faddish insistence on "natural foods" has brought the old art of bread baking back into importance. There is an almost sensuous pleasure about handling good bread sponge. It has a smoothness that may have been a kind of reward to the breadmakers of an earlier era, who regularly baked the family's bread, eight or nine loaves at a baking, and two or three bakings a week.

Verna said, "I never cared for salt-rising bread but I was a master hand at making yeast bread and I began early in life making it. We made our own yeast from hops grown in our own garden. Hops had to be picked in August. If the September winds blew on them it ruined them for yeast.

"Hops were used not only for breadmaking but also in medicinal ways. Hops poultices and hops pillows were thought to induce sleep for asthma sufferers. There were other uses, too. I remember well when in 1898 my husband's mother visited us she told of going to a neighbor's house to get some 'blue dye yeast.' This blue dye was the kind used to dye the uniforms worn by Northern soldiers in the Civil War. Also the blue used to dye yarn used in woven coverlets of that era. It never faded. Water, wheat bran, madder, and indigo were mixed for the yeast, then kept warm as one has to keep salt-rising bread if you expect it to 'come.' My mother-in-law said the dye was set on the hearth in an iron kettle until it fermented. She said when the bubbles were large on it and you blew on them and saw the colors of the rainbow in the bubbles, the dye was ready for use."

The Greenlees lived for thirty-nine busy years on a farm where the little white house still sits among its several farm buildings like a motherly little white Leghorn hen among her chicks. There Verna helped her husband with farm crops and care of livestock, poultry, garden, flowers. Her children were all born and reared there.

Verna's daughter, Marion Jeffries, wrote me of Verna. "In those years of devotion there was little time for self-expression. My mother tried to live her beliefs. She did not have channels of expression that are available today through organized community groups. Yet even then her horizons on the farm were unlimited. She was always searching and educating herself. I guess most farm women experience some of this conflict between the wife-mother relationship and the longing for self-expression."

If Verna experienced it, she won. Now she has straight white hair, disciplined by a comb which in moments of excitement or enthusiasm she takes out, runs through her hair, and puts back quickly. This happens often because Verna Greenlee has a youthful spirit and overflowing enthusiasms. Her eyes, which she describes as "Well, gray, I guess," are basically amber with both gray and blue in them. When she laughs they sparkle. "The little candle" is my private name for Verna, who throws her light so far.

We went on to a discussion of old-time rag carpets. "They were used in all the homes when I was growing up," Verna said. "Some women had looms and wove them at home. My mother saved all the old clothes for carpet rags. We ripped the seams apart, used every piece, and washed them. My mother dyed them." At the little country store where they "did the trading" they bought small amounts of Prussian blue and sugar of lead. "My mother boiled half of the light material in a bath made with sugar of lead to make it yellow. To get green she boiled some of the yellow in the Prussian blue bath.

"The dyed material was cut into strips about an inch wide. My mother spread an old sheet on the floor and every minute when we weren't busy at other work we sewed carpet rags together and wound them into balls. How glad we were when we got that done! The long, yard-wide woven strip of carpet was cut into lengths to fit the room for which the carpet was being made and the strips had to be sewed together with strong thread.

"Rag carpets had to be stretched very tight," Verna said. "The men folks were asked to help stretch and tack the edges all around. Folks used to put straw under the carpet. When we began getting newspapers we used several thicknesses of them. It helped keep out the cold and made the carpet feel softer to walk on. We heated our houses with stoves and by spring the carpets had to be taken up, ripped apart, and washed. Then all the sewing together, stretching, and tacking had to be gone through again."

Mrs. Gertrude Druyea Frier added to Verna's story. "I can remember how it was on a White County prairie farm where I was born in 1887 and where I lived until 1898, when my parents moved to Lafayette twenty-five miles away so their three little daughters could have more cultural and educational advantages.

"My mother always had a rag carpet in the making. Her big basket of materials was at hand for sitting-down tasks; tearing or sewing, or winding the rags. I learned in very small childhood there was a right way and a wrong way to sew carpet rags. The ends must be lapped over about three-fourths of an inch, then folded and sewed carefully so there will be no rough spots in the carpet.

"The carpet could be stretched with a carpet stretcher, which was a bar fitted with tacks and pulled by a lever. It was a bit of household equipment that was loaned from house to house as needed."

❧ BRINK STILLWATER SAID, standing in his barn door and thoughtfully watching a neighbor drive away, "Erzy must be doin' pretty well now. He's beginnin' to boast about his overdrafts."

Goodbye, Little Oscar

🐦 ON THE LIVING-ROOM FLOOR near the brass kettle in which geraniums have grown four feet tall this winter, something moved. Something drab-colored, about the size of an ordinary house spider. It could have crawled out of the soil in the geranium kettle, or could have been carried in on a stick of firewood. Who knows from where come the various bugs that appear in a rickety old farmhouse, casually, and at any time of year as if it were their house, too?

When I reached down to sweep the insect onto a cardboard it rolled into a tight little ball about the size of a ripe elderberry. Rolled up, it looked shinier and darker than when it was stretched out over its eight pairs of legs and trying to hunch its many-segmented body up onto the rug.

It was a wood louse, neither rare nor splendid, not in fact really classified as insect, but interesting because it is a descendant of the trilobite that existed five hundred million years ago in the Cambrian era. Any creature that has survived that long must have something to tell a new-comer.

My visiting wood louse had walked through dust under a chair. Now a tiny piece of paper, dusty and cobwebby, clung to its feet. Lying on its back, it played with the paper, passing it from one pair of legs to another and twirling it as a drum major twirls a baton.

The wood louse is terrestrial now, but from its ancient watery origin it has retained gills, and when selecting a dwelling place chooses preferably a dark, wet spot such as the underside of stones or old logs. It feeds on rotting wood and leaves, thus aiding nature in her thrifty use-up. The wood louse's defense against enemies is to roll up into an unappetizing little ball and hope the enemy will go away.

In the shallow enameled dish into which I dumped this guest for observation, it seemed unable to get itself back onto its wildly waving legs, though it never stopped trying.

It has some escape system, however: I left it there

while I went out to get dinner. When I came back the admirable wood louse was gone. Mysteriously, and leaving no trace.

꙳ IT'S SIMPLER to get a big, hard job done than a small, easy one that will wait until you get around to it. Anger or a sense of emergency will launch you on the big job, but getting started on the easy one depends on your self-discipline.

This I told myself while I nailed two loose boards back on the gate at Montie's house yesterday. I knew if I came away leaving those boards loose, the steers would finish tearing them off. Cattle are congenitally unable to resist this kind of joke making.

"What farmer hath put together let no cow hesitate to tear asunder" is their guideline. When we bought Ira's farm there was an old outdoor privy behind the washhouse, left there when Ira and Montie put in their bathroom.

The steers went to work immediately to demolish it. First they tore off the door. Then they knocked the building over and began pulling off the roof. Dick left them alone, curious to see how long it would take.

It took a year, and they did a thorough job of demolition.

꙳ IN THE RESEARCH from which he concluded, "There is no new thing under the sun," Ecclesiastes obviously did not consult any cattle. Farm cattle devote their energies to finding new things with which to keep their farm owner busy. Their resourcefulness in dealing with fences is well known, but their dealing with the old Kieffer pear tree in the springlot is new enough to have interested Ecclesiastes.

The pear tree is well over eighty years old and blooms every year. One winter a storm broke out half of it, vertically, but it rearranged itself to regain balance and went right on annually producing its greenish-brown pears that look hard as stone but if picked at the right time and properly ripened become yellow, red-flecked, and deliciously juicy. Every year the old pear tree blooms in lacy white.

In other years cattle running in the springlot paid no attention to the pear tree, but this year's playful, fat black Angus steers discovered the taste of pear bark as something new under the sun. They liked the new taste and began peeling off bark in long strips. To stop this I dragged two piles of apple brush close in around the pear's trunk. The steers watched interestedly and expressed their goodwill by following along and biting the brush. I wired it into place and left. The steers at once advanced on these emplacements as if apple brush tasted better than the ground corn and alfalfa hay they had been eating all winter. They removed the brush in far less time than it had taken me to put it there.

"I'll put a fence around the pear tree," Dick promised, and did it the next morning.

Later he told me, "There was not a steer in sight when I began but they were all there before I finished." He dug three postholes for the fence before he came in to dinner at noon. While he was taking his after-dinner nap, which he calls "getting my health back," the steers filled up the postholes. He had to dig them out again when he went back.

While he was setting the posts the steers dragged away the canvas bag in which he carried fence "steeples" and spilled them all out onto the grass. One steer grabbed the empty sack and ran off with it.

When he had set the woven wire into place against the posts, and was ready to fasten it there, he had to go creeping along the ground, hunting staples. For the steers, the sight of a man going on all fours was altogether too much newness under the sun. Their delight and curiosity overflowed. Four of them took hold of him, two pulling at his shirt sleeves, two removing his cap. He gathered up enough staples to finish the fence, despite their help. The steers congregated beside it and expressed a low opinion of the barricade. If it really keeps them out, it is going to be a new thing under the sun to all of us.

❧ As a matter of fact, Toby Nelson's famous egg coffee probably isn't any better than Grace Hanson's instant brewed in a percolator "and you absolutely can't tell it from real, brewed coffee" or the electric perk made in the farm's intelligent quick percolator that shuts itself off and keeps its mouth shut and the coffee hot for a long time afterward.

But there is a difference and the difference is important.

Toby's coffee is made over her mother's old recipe and the making is a ritual. For although on the surface Toby seems hard as a Kieffer pear, at heart she is a sentimental woman.

An only child, she grew up in the farmhouse in which she now lives. The farm is in Owen County, near Freedom, alongside unpredictable White River that some years goes on a rampage across the farms there and ruins their crops. From Toby's living-room windows all along the side of the house you can see the river and the new steel bridge that recently replaced the old covered one.

When Toby was a little girl, red-haired and impetuous, she played along the river. With one of her playmates, a boy who later became a famous college football player, she climbed into a barrel and let it roll dangerously down toward the river, as a game. One day when she was five years old and the cemetery caretaker came walking past the farm, Toby saw him and asked where he was going. "To clean off the cemetery," he said. "I'll go with you," she answered. She knew him; he worked for her grandmother in town. She went, without telling her parents, and had a happy time playing in the cemetery until noon, when the old man said, "Now, Toby, you've got to go home." She went cheerfully, not knowing her mother, sick with apprehension, had gone to bed and the neighbors had gathered to help her father drag the river for Toby's body.

Her mother was first to see the little girl walking nonchalantly home. Her father explained to her, in gentle, loving words, what she had done and in all the years afterward Toby tried to make up for it by tender care of her parents.

In time she became supervisor of a small new hospital and managed it ably for seventeen years, acquiring a reputation among the doctors as being "hard as nails." In those years she learned to know the doctors and nurses well, and most of the people in town. The hospital and the nurses' training school prospered under her rigorous management, but she was not ubiquitously popular. Early one morning on her way to the hospital office, she was in a car wreck that left her unable to walk. For a time she continued to manage the hospital from her desk. By installing ramps, railings, and walkers she made the Freedom house livable for a non-walker, and after her mother's death, retired there with a nurse friend, Hollis. The house is visited by great numbers of friends to whom Toby and Hollis always offer a cup of egg coffee.

Hollis has a small greenhouse, a vegetable garden, and flowers everywhere. Toby does the cooking, sitting on a tall stool. The two women are symbiotic.

Always, until New Year's Day when Dick and I stopped there, the coffee was already made, and poured into glass pots, keeping warm. That day there wasn't any, so Toby made it. The ritual takes so long and uses so many different utensils few people would bother with it. It is the recipe Toby's mother used.

In the kitchen, as in every room in the house, the face of her mother looks out affectionately from a framed photograph. It is the same photograph in every room. There is good humor and sympathy in it, and mellowness.

Beginning the coffee-making ritual, Toby sat down on her high stool at the snack bar, which is where her mother's old wood range was long ago. She began dipping ground coffee out of a big plastic bowl, counting the spoonfuls and putting them into a quart-sized, long-handled saucepan. She kept dipping and counting until finally I asked, "Are you measuring out coffee to use or just to see how much is in that bowl?" She smiled without answering or losing count. At "twelve" she carried the saucepan to the sink, where she washed two eggs and broke them on top of the ground coffee, then smashed the eggshells and dropped them in, too. Then she ran cold water over this whole mess and stirred it with a long-handled wooden spoon, worn at one side and slightly darkened.

"You have to use a wooden spoon," she told me, turning around to grin at me impishly. "This is the one Mom used."

All this time, in the gallon-sized white enamel coffeepot on the electric burner, water had been coming to a boil. The pot is decorated with Swedish designs and words that translate into something like "Coffee is the best of earth's good things."

"Anne Bradfute gave me this pot long ago," said Toby, whose name was originally Anna, "because she said she was tired of never having enough second cups for everybody."

The water must be boiling when you add the saucepan mess, but not thereafter allowed to boil. "When it comes barely to a boil you must draw it off, then push it back . . . off and back three times exactly," Toby explained, doing it. Eventually it is strained off into smaller glass pots, ready for drinking. A person staggering in, faint from coffee thirst, would still have to wait, even if he collapsed. However much she might love the straggler, Toby loved her mother more. The coffee-making ritual is her way of telling her mother, "I loved you then and I love you just as much now and when I make coffee we are together." And actually the egg coffee is every bit as good as Grace Hanson's instant brewed, or mine made in the intelligent percolator.

Goodbye, Little Oscar

❧ "It's HARD TO MAKE one kind of wood out of another," said John Cissna plaintively. We were looking at an ash chest someone wanted him to refinish as cherry.

In the paint-splattered gray work shirt his shoulders looked thin. His hands were worn and expressive. He is seventy-six years old and has worked hard all his life, some of the time for a farming uncle to whom he was merely a young boy who could be hired for a low wage, later in a furniture factory where he learned cabinetmaking.

He is skillful at his work, which is the repair and refinishing of furniture. His workshop is one large room in a small building almost directly behind his house and both are close to a heavily traveled highway. Sometimes he talks wistfully about getting a place in the country where there would be less noise and traffic. His workroom is crowded with machinery, tables, and equipment and supplies. All around are pieces of furniture . . . some pretty, some unusual, some grotesque, all waiting for the resurrecting touch of John Cissna's hands.

"You could stain this poplar cabinet, though, so it'd look almost like cherry," he added.

John Cissna never had much time and very little encouragement for going to school. He enjoys reading, especially the Bible and of it especially the Old Testament. He has endured some injustices which he still resents and has a few memories bitter as grapefruit rind, but he never has become self-pitying. He lives by a philosophy of thorny realism and thoroughly enjoys political or religious discussions with his customers. He tells jokes and asks questions and makes wry comments.

Once, going to bring home a table he had refinished for us, we took him a package of frozen beef, as any farmer might do for a neighbor who doesn't butcher. It surprised him. He said, "Nobody ever gave me anything before."

With educational opportunity he might have gone into a profession involving public speaking, for although he does not have a deep, dramatic voice, he is an excellent mimic. Mimicking, he said, "Women bring me furniture here to finish and tell me, 'Now, this is an old family piece and I want it as soon as you can get it done because my club's going to meet at my house.' And then if I hurry and get it out, half the time they ain't in any hurry to come after it." He has developed a way to deal with them. "A woman brought me a big old walnut bureau once," he said, relishing the memory, "and told me she wanted it right away, it was a family treasure, been in the family forever, and all that. I got it done and called her and she didn't come. I called her a couple more times and finally I called her and said, 'Well now, I've got this bureau painted blue like you said you wanted it.' She just screamed and was out here right away for it."

He would have enjoyed being a preacher. He has taught a Sunday-school class at a country church for the past seven years and says with quiet pride, "My class tells me they've learned more about the Bible than they ever knew before." He especially likes the Book of Daniel and thinks the Book of Ezekiel predicts all of today's problems.

"What does 'replenish' mean?" he asked me, seeming glad to sit idle. I sat down on a broken chair admiring a little cradle he had just finished. It rocks and also swings and I was thinking how pretty a baby would look in it. "When Adam was told to 'replenish' the earth," continued John Cissna, persistent as a person digging old varnish out of a crack, "did that mean there had been people on earth before Adam and they disappeared?"

Like many earnest Bible students, he doesn't attach much importance to the probability that the English version of the Bible is a translation from another translation, or that some of it came from old scrolls and currently there are several different versions in the English language.

He can quote a great deal of it, and probably ponders over it while working alone in his shop.

He interrupted his catechism to show us the treasures that are not for sale and are kept in an old poplar cupboard that has glass panes in its doors and would be pretty if he refinished it.

One of the treasures is a box of seashells, from which he picked up a sand-dollar test. The powdery gray sand spilled out of it as he held it up and explained its religious significance. The five petal-like slits that make this shell look like a decorated 4-H cookie represent a man's body and the nailprints on hands and feet, he explained. "If I broke this shell," he said devoutly, "I would find the five birds, symbolic of the dove that appeared when Christ was baptized and the Voice said, 'This is my beloved son.' "

Here he interrupted himself abruptly to give me a quick, sharp glance and asked, "You believe in evolution, don't you?"

I said yes, and he answered firmly, "Well, I don't. I believe the creation happened just exactly the way it tells me in the Bible." He invited us to visit his Sunday-school class.

John Cissna is a good man, realistic in most ways, not ungenerous or argumentative and not sentimental. He has rigid ideas of right and wrong and his religion sustains him. He has lived honorably by it and, dying, will undoubtedly be comforted by it. What else can one ask of religion?

While I listened to him I was thinking how glad I am that other countries do not feel obligated to send missionaries here to convert people like John Cissna. His faith is sufficient to him just as it is.

※ "This is Will Hauser's farm," Dick said to my sister Grace and me. It was Sunday afternoon and we were on our way home from a farm several miles beyond the Hauser place. We drove slowly, admiring the farm. Apple trees were in bloom in the orchard that had been pruned earlier in spring. Fields were green, well groomed, fences clean and in good repair.

The small old brick house sat on the crest of a low, grassy hill, recently mowed. All the barns and sheds, even the one that leans perceptibly toward the woods, were in neat repair. The whole farm had the cherished look characteristic of a farm owned by a thrifty Dutch farmer.

While we were slowly passing, Will came out in his work clothes to do the barn work and, assuming we were coming to visit, waited for us to drive up to the barn.

"Come in," he exclaimed heartily. "We've got a cake and a ham we just started on at noon today. You women can help my wife get supper." When we explained we couldn't stay he insisted we come in for a while, anyway. His wife would like to meet us, he said, leading the way toward the house.

Will is eighty-two years old, a small man with keen,

searching eyes in a sun-wrinkled face. He walks with a vigorous long stride and sees nothing remarkable about his helping a neighbor yard logs all day.

His wife, Selma, opened a door on the long side porch and led us into the living room. Her eyes are gentian blue, her cheeks pink and youthful. She laughs at all of Will's jokes and blushes at his compliments. She blushed when he told us about the man who said, "Will, I've just kissed your wife," and was told, "Well, I wouldn't want a wife nobody would want to kiss."

It was early for most women to be thinking of spring housecleaning, but Selma had thought of it and already had it half done. "I always start with the yard," she told us. "I've finished all the raking and burning outside. Now I'm ready to start on the inside."

The house, tidy as a cat's freshly washed fur, has always been a Hauser home, built by Will's uncle, who lived in it many years. Will and Selma had been married seven and a half years before they moved into it and have been there ever since. In October they will have been married fifty-seven years. They have eight children and twenty grandchildren. Will said in his quick way of speaking, "I started givin' each grandchild five dollars at Christmas and now it costs me a hundred dollars every Christmas." Selma laughed contentedly.

The ceilings of the one-story house are high. It has electricity and modern plumbing but is heated by fuel-oil stoves. The living room is comfortably furnished with a bed, sofa, upholstered chairs, radio, stove, and a parlor organ burdened with photographs. Wherever there was space in the room for a photograph, Selma had put one. There were framed photographs on the walls, on the mantel of the closed-up fireplace. The day being mild, there were photographs on the unburning fuel-oil stove, mostly photographs of their children and grandchildren.

Will began driving a Model-T Ford in 1915. He still drives his car to town and to the little country church near their farm, or wherever he and Selma want to go. Last year, at eighty-one, he had no trouble getting a license.

He likes to discuss politics but says, "I'm not set in my ways, politically." Having made his own way financially with very little help, he has scant respect for the philosophy of comfort as something society owes everybody. He began farming when horses supplied the power for farm machinery. He fed his horses well, took good care of them, and worked them hard.

He reads the Bible faithfully, believes it literally, exactly as it is written, questioning nothing, retaining all the old words. Basing his opinion on it, he thinks the world is "about four or five thousand years old." His sister-in-law, who heard him say that, told him gently, "I believe it is much older." He made no attempt to change her opinion, and offered no revision of his own. I think he feels that religion, like farming, must be pursued within a strict schedule of devotion, from which a man must not deviate.

FOR A WHILE there was a little white dog that sometimes visited the farm with his young owners. A little West Highland terrier with shaggy, rough hair hanging down like bangs in front of his eager black eyes. He had a dark knob of a nose and nice sharp white teeth that grabbed but never bit hard into the hand that stroked or fed him. He loved being played with vigorously, and could hardly bear to waste time eating when he visited the farm although he always drank thirstily as soon as he arrived from the long ride.

His farm days were full of interesting things to do. He kept the farm poultry in a state of baffled unrest and rout. The geese went out beyond sight into the hilltop pasture when he came. The guineas, peafowls, and half-cocks ceased to come down to the kitchen to beg for brown bread and hamburger. The Bantams fled squawking when little white Oscar went up with the men to the barnlot.

But when cattle were near the barn, the dog perked up his little pointed ears on his squarish head, looked at the cattle, and fled. When the steers gathered at the feed trough, Oscar sought refuge on the tractor seat and waited for Dick to come back out of the barn. Since nobody saw him get up onto the seat, nobody knew how many desperate leaps it took to gain that high, safe place.

While the family sat eating meals from the round table in the kitchen, Oscar put his front feet against the big glass door and scratched, looking in, eager and appealing. But he never pushed his way in without being invited. In every way he loved the farm. He was only a few months old and therefore did not understand the menace of automobiles and was killed by one, soon after a joyous visit to the farm. His sorrowing young owners brought him back to the farm and buried him in the front yard near the wildlife corner, beside Rose the farm Collie. It seemed the natural and comforting thing to do.

❧ THE HINDUSTAN CHURCH in Monroe County is like Uncle Bent Stanger's locust fence post: "It'll last a hundred years and then turn to iron and last a hundred more." The church is now in its second hundred years and its second building. Architecturally like many Midwest rural churches, it is a one-room, small, white-painted frame building flanked by its cemetery. Unlike some, it has a bell, which is rung for Sunday-night services.

It has never had a large congregation and is not likely ever to have, for membership potential is limited in the non-agricultural rural community around Hindustan. Like a hardy perennial, the church goes dormant from time to time, but somebody or some group always revives it. At present it is the special project of the Hindustan Women's Boosters Club, of which June Fulford is president much of the time.

Hindustan is not a town, not even a village, although in 1853, when the area was Charles Corr's farm, he hoped it would become a town. He hired a surveyor from the county seat eleven miles south to lay it out into twelve lots, complete with alleys. For a while Hindustan had a blacksmith shop, a grocery store, a few offices and shops, and a church. The church served two congregations, Baptist and Church of Christ, on alternate Sundays.

Mr. Corr evidently liked the name Hindustan without knowing its East Indian pronunciation. The little village, of which now only the church and a decrepit grocery building remain, and both are replacements of the original buildings, is known among local people simply as " 'Dustan" and the name rhymes with "roostin'."

The hilly, broken land, only a few miles from a large state forest reserve, has some orchards, some truck patches, and some small farms, but mostly its residents work at town jobs. They live in modern houses along the road, which is the old State Highway 37. They have rural electricity, city water and gas lines, modern plumbing, TV's, radios, telephones, and cars. Their children go to junior high and high school in the metropolitan system in the county-seat town. Some go on to the university there, some into business and professional careers.

The Sunday-evening congregation is usually around twenty-five. Currently the minister is a young man engaged in theological extension work at the university and takes no regular salary. The evening offering is used as church and minister decide.

The Hindustan Boosters have other charitable and community projects. When it was organized about fifteen years ago, in one of the church's dormancies, the club's announced purpose was threefold: "To serve the welfare of the community, to see after the church's financial interest, and to give practical help in emergencies." Such as burnouts, funerals, sickness.

Even in its dormancies, the church has inspired the people into imaginative effort such as giving a home-talent play for the benefit of special charities. It gives special programs at Thanksgiving, Christmas, and summertime homecomings. Former residents come from long distances to the homecomings.

In its present era of bloom, the church has achieved electricity and gas, a tiny kitchen built into a front corner of its large one room, a carpet, and enough used songbooks to supply all of its long, wooden benches. It has a piano and keeps it tuned.

Last year the women decided to give a Thanksgiving appreciation dinner to all the church helpers and any other guests who cared to come. "We can feed everyone that comes," said June Fulford confidently when the minister told her, almost apologetically, there would be

twenty-five from town. Eventually there were a hundred
and ten who partook of a dinner that included roast duck,
turkey, baked ham, chicken, oyster dressing and "other
dressing," mashed potatoes, green beans, pickles and
relishes, cranberry sauce, fruit salad, tossed salad, hot
rolls, pies—"mostly pumpkin, but some chess, custard,
apple, mince"—and cakes, including a decorated birthday cake for the minister, persimmon pudding, coffee,
tea, and iced soft drinks. When one young man asked
June jokingly, "Why do I have such a small plate?" she
took it away and substituted a large meat platter, filled,
and told him, "I want this all eaten."

After dinner the guests visited, reminisced, walked
over the grounds admiring the improvements, and everyone felt the church had never held a happier gathering.

Several years earlier, when June Knight dropped
out of high school to marry her jobless, untrained boy
friend Willard Fulford, her neighbors and teachers regretted it; June was too young, they said, too bright and
promising to marry so soon. Since her mother's death
when June was only a child she had been housekeeper for
her father and three brothers. Their farm was a grudging
little space at the foot of a hill, with a rocky creek running across the back of it. June's father was amiable, but
not ambitious and in that time and situation unlikely ever
to be able to offer much to his children. He welcomed
the young people who sometimes gathered at his house for
play-parties and square dances and ice-cream suppers.
They played singing games like "Three Old Maids" and
"Tideo." When they sang "Skip to M' Lou" they in-
serted their own homemade verse that they liked: "Never
git to 'Dustan, swingin' on a gate." They did square

dances not because it was a fad, but because it was the only kind of dancing they knew. It was robust and exciting, and everybody danced, the old as well as the young.

Neither June nor her boy friend, whom everyone called Bubb, was accustomed to luxury or even easy living. They were confident they could get along. They started housekeeping in a little shack of a house in the community where both had lived all their lives. Their first baby was born within a year and eventually they had twelve children, ten of whom lived to become adults.

Somehow June and Bubb did get along. They enjoyed life and made it more enjoyable for other people. Through the Depression, Bubb worked at whatever unskilled work he could get, sometimes in the city forty miles distant. They took the hard times with the good ones in a kind of lighthearted earnestness. They participated in school affairs because they wanted to make sure their children gave and received their share of whatever there was. Sometimes the school appreciated June's forthright advice and sometimes it didn't.

Eventually June and Bubb bought a little farm, not far from her father's home. They designed and economically built their own practical, attractive modern home on it. Later they set a used trailer near it and rented it to university students who needed inexpensive housing. June took a helpful, maternal interest in the students, and many of them, after graduating and going on to careers in distant places, have come back just to visit.

Some of the time while she still had some children in school, June worked in an automatic laundry, where her native business acumen and a genuine interest in people increased the popularity of the place. Their children finished high school, got jobs, married early, had children of their own. Some moved into other states, some built modern new homes along the road in the area.

As her home duties decreased, June steadily took on more community responsibility. By being herself unaffectedly and giving herself generously, she has made herself a person of distinction and personal worth.

That probably is the finest service offered by the little country churches and explains why they continue to survive . . . to give people a reason for exerting their own ingenuity and imagination, their own material and spiritual resources, and then to share the sense of accomplishment.

⩙ SAID BRINK STILLWATER, bona fide farmer, after attending a symphony concert he hadn't really wanted to hear, "Well, I think maybe music is the fourth human need. You know: Food, shelter, the daily newspaper, and then music."

Poem in a Sunlit Frame

🦅 RED LOBELIA, also called cardinal flower, is in bloom now in the grassy waterway along Beanblossom Road. It is a perennial, said to be poisonous to livestock, but so beautiful it is in danger of becoming extinct from over-picking.

Its blue counterpart, called simply lobelia, is in bloom, too, in the ditch beside the long driveway down to Ira's. In either color, lobelia is a message of late summer. When it blooms you can see the first barely perceptible yellow across the wooded hillsides, as significant as the nod or secret hand gesture by which a farmer communicates his bid to a livestock auctioneer. It is coincident with the first glimpses of orange-colored school buses along country roads. After that, even if you have no children to get onto the school bus, the days have a different feeling.

꙳ IN THE AFTERNOON of a day in late summer I went to the wilderness to interview a snail. It has always seemed to me that the snail's calcareous spiral is a classic shape, with poetic and philosophic import.

You can count on finding a live snail and the white, empty shells of these gastropods in the woods. They are sensitive to cold, and when the time comes to deposit their eggs, thirty to a hundred at a time, they seek out moist, protected places.

I went down the first hillside, crossed the creek near a huge walnut tree, and climbed up the opposite hill to a wide limestone outcropping where I like to sit. Under the ledge something that has an underground cave had dug itself another entrance. The earth was freshly piled up there. It was a good spot for a secret house, the sense of uninterruption seemed luxurious even to me. Looking down the hill, I could see the creek's banks, surprisingly deep for so small a creek. I could see the big fallen oak from whose dead roots every year chanterelle mushrooms spring like saucer-sized yellow petunias.

Near me were ferns and a gaggle of wild gooseberry bushes. I had brought a small microscope and pencils and paper, and on the way had picked up three empty shells and one with a live snail in it. Commonplace and exquisite, these are as much a part of the woods narrative as ferns or wildflowers are.

When the snail is alive, its mobile home is pale brown and white, sometimes mottled and often verging wetly on an unimpressive lavender. My interview snail was drably earth-colored, but when I laid it on the stone the late-afternoon sunlight gave it brightness. I picked it up firmly to examine under the microscope, and the snail put out a glutenous, single foot which felt cold against my thumb and exerted a vigorous suction pull. Simultaneously a slimy lubricant flowed in waves, like water, down the foot. When the snail is free, this foot drags the shell along in what seems like an aimless rambling. On a dry surface, such as the porch floor where I have seen these trails, they make a tangled record of the snail's travels, and glisten as if written in raw egg white.

A newly hatched snail is one and a half swirls big, and symmetrical. Very soon the left-side organs atrophy but those on the right continue to grow and the live snail pushes forward in the increasing shell. This pushing and resisting creates the spiral pattern. The unhardened rim of the shell is white with the look of purity characteristic of seashells, and the shell itself, wide and open at the outer end, looks like a cornucopia.

The snail makes no sound, obviously is not bothered by claustrophobia, has an acute sense of touch and possibly a sense of smell. The eyes are on the ends of the two larger of its four hollow tentacles, and the viscid body is a masterpiece of packaging and foldability. When danger requires, the tentacles, eyes and all, can be quickly drawn back into the shell.

Unable to pull itself free, the snail retired into its shell and cast out an excretion, a dark, shining, worm-shaped loop, surprisingly long.

Every snail is both male and female and therefore impregnates other snails and is in turn impregnated by others. So there seems to be no likelihood of the woods running out of snails although casualties are high. Many are eaten by birds and animals. The larvae of glowworms are said to eat small snails. Woods fires, floods, sharp temperature changes, falling rocks and trees destroy many. Yet enough survive that if you have to have one, you can go to the woods confident of finding it. When the interview was over I laid the snail on the ground and watched it move slowly away to its private affairs.

The spiral shape, as exemplified in the snail's delicate shell, is the pattern of evolution. Within it life keeps moving forward against resistance, and thus, although it returns near to the starting point, it never touches it, closing to form a static circle.

The circle is the shape of eternity, but the eternal spiral is the shape of evolution.

🦅 THE SCHOOL BUS rolled orangely along the road this morning as I walked there. The bus driver waved, some of the children waved and smiled, and I waved back. We went our separate ways and never have I wished more ardently that I could write poetry.

For poetry can speak condensedly, in code, unassailable within its eloquent tough husk, and everyone interprets according to his own beliefs. The bus passed and in a moment was out of sight beyond the curve of the east road.

Poem in a Sunlit Frame

Youth is a poem in a sunlit frame. The form changes continually as new groups move forward in their bright vehicle, but the poem remains the same.

The world of the young is larger than the adult world because it contains all that can be, all the unmade decisions and rejections. Theirs is a world whereof the outer end is open like a snail's cornucopia, and from its intensified light, life emerges into a light diffused over a greatly widened timescape. That morning these children were being borne gaily along toward the larger opening, and by the time they emerge a pattern will be determined by the forces that shape human life; the person, the environment, the circumstance.

It is inherent in humankind that each group, while it occupies the frame, will try to change the existing order. Youth always sincerely believes it is more honest, more enlightened than the generation ahead, and more able to initiate the perfect order. And thus convinced, and thus trying, each group in its turn moves out of the frame and into the wider, less focused light of the outer world, beyond the cornucopia.

People have wondered, but never learned, whether the groups now standing outside the frame in the wider horizon and looking with tenderness, pity, anger, or hope toward the small sunlit group within the frame, may ever return to that sunlit place.

And those young, when they are looking back from their widened, diffused horizon, will they accord their successors the tolerance and listening they now demand from their predecessors? No, they will not; for that is not the way of life, or of youth, or of poetry, either.

There is something infinitely beautiful and poignant about this poem. I look at today's youth with curiosity, with admiration sometimes tinged with pity, sometimes with envy. The group outside must always listen to the voice of youth as to voices singing at dusk from some high hill, or voices dramatized and made harmonious by being carried across the water. Never as the voice of one leaning above a deep, empty well and shouting down into it, so that the sound comes back hollow and ghostly.

I think probably the most accurate poem about youth in its sunlit morning is the poignant one composed for me by my four-year-old son, telling me how things were going to be "when you are as little as I am, and I am as big as you."

⊻ "IT'S THE YOUNG PEOPLE who buy these old things like carnival glass and the big, ornate vegetable dishes; they're crazy about that stuff," said Vivien, presiding hospitably over her antique shop in friendly little Waveland.

"Why?"

"They say they have seen so much plastic stuff they yearn for something they think is real, and good. You know, the sturdy old virtues, some of the ugly old things. They say these things seem genuine to them."

⊻ THE WATER JUG Dick takes on the tractor on haying days is a white plastic gallon-sized container that originally contained washing concentrate used by dairy farmers. Dick likes it because it can be filled with water and frozen solid in the farm freezer. On hot days in the hayfield, sun melts the ice just fast enough to provide always one cold drink around a chunk of ice. A leather strap, looped through the handle, hangs it from the tractor. Usually the strap is dependable but a few weeks ago it let go and the jug fell off. The tractor ran over it, squashing it into an interesting new art form but not disabling it, so it continued to go to the field. I look with respect on this battered item when I wash and refill it to put into the freezer. I have the feeling that five thousand years from now, when archeologists are digging up the artifacts of our proud, tumultuous society, the plastic jug may be what's there to represent us.

⤋ "YOU ARE THE REAL DROPOUTS of society, you people there on the family farms," wrote a young woman from her home in a fast-growing city. She grew up on an Indiana farm and became a newspaper reporter, working with high-school journalists.

"More accurately I should say the old America, family life, the individual tribe, the relative isolation of a family that makes it on its own with a little help from neighbors . . . these have dropped out.

"Today American society and culture resides and is shaped in the urban areas, which no one likes and against which the youth are revolting. But look at the federal programs, our national problems, and the whole growing discontent and you find these directed at or deriving from the concrete habitat of the major cities. Small-town America is on the way to becoming the dreadful plastic drive-in, drive-out the cities have dissolved into.

"The youth are dropping out in an attempt to reconstruct something they never knew. They don't know how to give it the solidarity and worth the family farm had, run by a real farmer and a real farmwife. I feel sorry for the youth because they won't make it. They were born in too much plastic.

"The family farm, the small farmers, are the dropouts that stayed in when the rest of America dropped out."

❧ FARMERS WHO MACHINE-PICKED a heavy corn crop last year have now taken disk and flail chopper to the fields and cut up the winter-bleached stalks in preparation for what Purdue University calls "the plow-down." This fast new system of applying fertilizer from a truck with drag chain and fan, according to the need indicated by individual field test, is part of the new farming.

Later, planting corn, they will apply granular fertilizer through flexible hose on the corn planter, and will also side-dress the crop. Some will put on, additionally, a liquid fertilizer.

Local farmers, breaking the ground, use three-, four-, or five-bottom plows, and each bottom cuts a furrow fourteen inches wide. Any size farm now requires fast, powerful machinery, which is expensive to own or rent, and noisy. Basically farmers like this big machinery because it is an extension of a man's own land-manipulating reach. Big farms require powerful machinery to get the work done, and then the machinery requires more land to pay for the big machinery. So the cycle expands, becoming continually less personal, and people say gloomily, "The family farm is gone."

But in the broad pattern of human existence, the yearning for earth contact is inherent. It boils up persistently like the "rolling, tumbling boil that cannot be stirred down," as the jelly directions say.

❧ THE FAMILY FARM has joined the list of endangered species, but there is reason to believe it need not become extinct. It will be a bleak day for society if the time comes when the last family farm, like the last passenger pigeon, is kept in a zoo and the keeper tells visitors, "This is the last. When this one dies, there won't be any more."

For aside from its limited contribution of food and fiber, the small farm has always contributed something valuable to industrial and academic society. Daniel Webster probably had it in mind when he said, "When tillage begins, other arts follow. The farmers are therefore the foundations of human civilization."

The family farm's best crop is its influence on youth. Being more personal than the large farms, it produces a harvest of the spirit. Its value is in the way it promotes self-reliance, ingenuity in meeting emergencies, practical use of materials available at hand; in the way it encourages youth to accept responsibility, act on it, and abide honorably by the consequences of having acted on it; and in the way, whether deservedly or in illusion . . . people regard the farm as a place of peace and quietness.

So what can the family farm do to promote survival, other than wring its hands and lament, or stand around with a finger in its mouth whimpering for federal aid?

It can express itself; a farm that is not self-reliant and hopeful is not a good farm or well managed. To survive it has to be both. The family that asks too much

outside help is not a good farm family. Self-reliance, sometimes to the point of obstinacy, is the core of its survival,
and essential to its health.

But in expressing itself, the small farm must not
cut itself off from realistic contact with the world. This
has been tried in the past, never with success or per-
manence. Notable examples are the Brooks Farm experiment of intellectuals on 192 Massachusetts acres around
1841, and George Rapp's New Harmony experiment in
Indiana around 1825. With high ideals and unnatural
rules to enforce them, the Shakers in Kentucky failed because they tried to make a religion out of occupational
self-sufficiency.

A family farm must operate on free expression of
individual opinion, but its members . . . its families if
there are as many as two or three working together . . .
must be genuinely compatible and they must be farmers
because they prefer to be.

Farm youth must be trained and educated to leave
the farm if they choose to. It may be the best contribution they can make, for even if the farm, or group of
farms, can make itself wholly self-sustaining in point
of food and fuel, the family farm still requires a cash
income, and sometimes this has to come from something
other than farm crops. Modern life, of which the family
farm is inescapably a part, requires certain social com-
pliances, such as payment of taxes, purchase and upkeep
of machinery, education for everybody, and the farm's
share of assistance to needs outside of the farm.

Farmers can never stop and let themselves feel
righteous and fulfilled. For this civilization, like man
himself, is unfinished and still evolving. It has a consider-

able way to go yet before it is all plowed and worked down, seeded and ready to be "laid by."

🕊 WHEN POWER MOWERS and electricity became available in the remote places, farm life was made easier, also more vulnerable to invasion by land developers. From then on, the automobile being already ubiquitous, anybody who could get a few acres in the country could have a job in town, and town conveniences in the country, with no chores except to mow the yard. Or he could "run a few cattle," keep a dog and riding horse, and cook outdoors.

It became a test of devotion for the small farmer to keep his acres for tilling, rather than sell them at development prices, and let his farm be cut up into little pieces like chicken for a pot pie.

🕊 A FEW YEARS AGO a teacher asked the county agent, Joe Sylvester, where she could take her class to see a real farm. He asked us to let them come here. We liked the visitors and they liked the farm. The word spread and more came. By now we have around six hundred child visitors a year.

They come in late April and May, when the youngness of earth is everywhere evident on the farm. The children walk gaily in this newness of life and merge with it.

The visit requires around an hour and a half, and the farm can accommodate a wagonload of children, thirty-five to forty-five, at a time. Since there are at most only sixty-one days in April and May, and some are Sundays and some are rainy days, the visiting creates a tight schedule for a corn-planting farmer. But we feel this is a service a small family farm can give, and besides we enjoy it, too.

It is astonishing how many children, even those from a small city, have never seen milk come from a cow's udder or a hen brooding eggs on a nest, or heard unhatched chicks pecking the pipped shell, or compared the shapes and sizes of eggs from different species of fowl. Many have never fed ducks from their hands and felt the sidewise, rivery movement of the wide flat bill gathering up the grains, or stroked the shaggy coat of a docile calf, or watched honey bees stream in and out of a hive.

For the most part, the poultry and animals on this farm are unafraid and tame. The teachers tell the children beforehand to be quiet and not chase things. One class approached the peacock in such complete silence he was suspicious, suddenly cried "yowp!" and fled. The initial silence soon gives way to a lively, explorative curiosity.

One year the steers on the other side of the yard fence became wildly excited at the arrival of a class of Catholic children. The cattle ran jumping and kicking across the field, while young, lovable Sister Regina Claire stood at the fence and laughed heartily. "If those cows ever give milk again it'll be a miracle!" she exclaimed, and the farmer told her gently, "It will indeed, Sister; those cows are steers."

As today's farms go, this is a small farm, 239 acres of pasture, tillable fields, and woods. Some of the children in their thank-you letters referred to the small hilltop woods charmingly as "your forest." They write these

letters themselves, and illustrate them with crayon drawings of what they saw on the farm. The letters are sufficient reward to us, but it is also flattering to be recognized
by some of the little visitors later when we meet them in
other places. As once when a car passed us in town and
a child leaned out and cried, "There's Mr. Peden! Hello,
Mr. Peden!"

The children come from schools and kindergartens,
public and private. Some from the Wheeler Rescue Mis-
sion of Indianapolis, which has a summer camp near
here and does a noble service with inner-city children.
Some have come from a city church project which brings
underprivileged children from cities, mostly from Chicago and mostly black children. We have also had mentally handicapped visitors.

The routine developed spontaneously and is simple:
We show the children what we have. On nearly every
visit there is some non-routine incident. Some years there
is a gentle cow willing to let Dick milk a stream from her
udder into a child's hand; or one that will let him set the
children, one at a time, on her back. One year they saw a
rabbit sitting beside her fur-lined nest in the ground and
one year there was a baby rabbit they could hold. Sometimes they take turns sitting on the seat of the well-braked
tractor and holding the steering wheel. The tractor always
figures prominently in their thank-you illustrations.

One year we visited a creek-bottom field in flood,
and went across the covered bridge. Another time the
children discovered the old weathered empty bones of a
cow that had died long ago, and they pounced on them
with the joy of an anthropologist discovering bronto-
saurus remains.

The visitors arrive on a school bus (thus covered

by school insurance) or in cars driven by teachers and
mothers. They come out of the vehicles like chickens let
out of the henhouse. Oftentimes they have been assigned
to separate groups, differentiated by name tags cut in the
shapes of different animals, or in different colors, and it
is amusing to hear a mother demand, "All the pigs over
here now, beside me."

For all their eagerness, the children are well-be-
haved. They enjoy telling us about themselves. A little
girl told me, "Do you know something? I'm four years
old." A boy listening said, "I'm four years old, too. And
do you know what? My birthday begins on Christmas."
It does, too. His mother makes him feel that Christmas
is a preliminary to a birthday on the twenty-sixth.

A little black girl with the Friendly City group at
once clasped me around the knees and said homesickly,
"I want to stay with you." While we walked through the
woods she told me about her mother and her mother's job,
her mentally retarded brother, and her street address in
Chicago.

The children are always interested in the horses and
mules and would like to ride. Beef production being the
farm's livelihood, there are usually around one hundred
and fifty cattle, mostly steers, but there are always a few
cows with small calves and there is a bull. Often he wears
blinders, harmless things that do not prevent him from
grazing or seeing the ground, but make it difficult for
him to break through fences to visit the neighbor's cows
or quarrel with the neighbor's bull. In all years the bull is
gentle, but the children are not taken near him. They
remember him and his blinders, which they call his spec-
tacles, and draw delightful crayon pictures of him.

They see Bernie Goodman's white beehives at the

edge of the hilltop woods and once when Dick attempted to tell them about bees a couple of the children helped with the information.

There are usually some goslings and young mallards for the children to touch or feed out of their hands, and some adult geese sitting on nests on baled hay in the machinery shed. The sitting goose stretches forth her neck to its full length and hisses, showing her long, pointed tongue and the serrated edges of her bill. The children like to see the big eggs in the nest. One little boy asked Dick, "When will the goose hatch?" Dick said, "The goose won't hatch until school is out." The boy asked in quick astonishment, "Does the goose go to school?"

The children happily collect souvenirs—corncobs, feathers, ear corn, insects, bones. One year the men of Company I had groomed the mules for a parade, trimming manes and hoofs in the machinery shed and left the parings. The children eagerly gathered up all the parings and a little girl wrote, "I can always remember the smell of the farm by the smell of the mules tow nails."

One boy happily carried home a fat green worm. One found a turtle and was going to take it home, but, to my relief, the teacher convinced him it would be better for the turtle to stay on the farm.

The high point of the visit is the ride in the sparrow-splashed, tractor-pulled wagon. It goes out through the barnlot, across the terraces. The more it jolts, the better they like it. There they can be as noisy as they wish. Afterward they write, "I liked the bumpy ride. It was fun," and draw pictures of themselves in the wagon.

The wagon is a hard-working farm implement. When it is not hauling schoolchildren it hauls feed from the barn to the cattle troughs. It is therefore always bedded with bales of hay or a deep layer of ground corn. The teachers and parents climb into it graciously, without complaint. When they get back from the ride the children take off their shoes and pour out the corn. On the ride they can dip out handfuls to feed the cattle that gather around. The wagon is like a zoo in reverse; from a safe enclosure the children can pet or feed the animals.

Some classes bring their midmorning refreshments of milk and cookies and eat on the hilltop in the pasture, from which there is a wide, lovely view of wooded hills.

Like the cast in a play, each class includes expectable characters; always the one or two you yearn to keep; always the timid one; the rebel; the explorer; always the poetic one who will give you a fresh view of your cherished farm, like the little boy who in pure ecstasy ran around and around the corncrib singing one word, "farm, farm, farm, farm," over and over into a poem. There is the one who weeps, the blasé one. One said, "Ugh, that smell!" and another, "I wouldn't want to live on a farm, ever." In one class two little girls told Dick they were going to marry him. From another class one little girl cried and wanted to stay with me, although her mother had driven one of the cars. In their letters they write touching, childishly frank messages: "I love you, do you love me?" or "Please call me," and give their phone numbers and addresses. The Catholic children write, "I pray for you." One little girl wrote, "I liked the everything!"

After the wagon ride, Dick takes them into the barn to show them the little floating swamp in the silo, which to me seems like a small miracle, but interests the children less than it interests the parents and teachers.

At the last he gives each child a length of baler

twine from the collection he has cut from hay bales and hung over a gate in the barn. The children come out of the barn and use the twine for jumping ropes. One little boy wrote, "Thank you for the rope. I am going to use it to tie up my little brother." One of the greatest compliments came from a little girl who climbed up on a mound of earth that serves as a loading chute and suggested brightly, "Let's start all over again."

I always wish, for the children's sake, we had more kinds of animals. But I always comfort myself by believing that someday probably these brief visits will have an influence in something the children do, even if they remember it dimly or even only subconsciously. A farm is good or valuable according to the memories it yields.

⅄ MRS. SKIRVIN, a minister's wife who teaches first grade at the Marlin school, brought fifty-nine children and some mothers and teachers to the farm one morning. Rain had started at daybreak, so we had assumed they would not keep their appointment. Dick was in his white-house oiling mule harness. From the back-porch window I saw the corner of the silently arrived school bus and went out. Children were emerging into the downpour.

"It wasn't raining at the school," said Mrs. Skirvin plaintively.

"But it looked gray," admitted an attractive young mother.

Mrs. Skirvin had already overcome the big hurdle of getting a school bus that late in June. Her brother-in-law drives it. She is a woman whose considerable natural tact is increased from thirty-nine years of teaching and I don't know how many years of being a minister's wife. "Could we just drive up to the barn and let them see something, anything?" she suggested, smiling and full of faith.

And behold, maybe due to the influence of the Reverend Mr. Skirvin, when the bus had driven up to the barn and stopped where the children could get out "in the dry" as Dick suggested, the rain abruptly stopped.

The sun came out. The peacock spread out his full glory, the mallards paraded in single file, the Bantams flew out, Company I's mules heehawed at the pasture gate, and the steers gathered around like children around a story hour.

The children discovered, for themselves, the wonderful possibilities of a pulley in a tree. They discovered corncobs, feathers. They even got a wagon ride. Not the usual one bumping over terraces up the hill, past the beehives and among the cattle. That pasture was too soft for the tractor wagon. They got a ride along the stoned driveway down to Ira's farm, where they saw a box turtle, saw buckeye trees and the hedge where wildlife travels in safety and bluebirds and goldfinches appear. They saw the steers down there and a shallow pond and other things not usually included on the visits.

Shortly after they left the rain began again, throwing thunder around recklessly. It rained all afternoon. Surely it was enough to give the Reverend Mr. Skirvin a fine Sunday text: "Ask and you shall receive . . ."

THE LATE-NOVEMBER WIND came downhill like someone having important news to tell and having rushed from great distance to tell it. The excitement was contagious. Dry maple leaves, long since fallen and settled into heaps in sheltered spots, now stirred and rustled as if exclaiming, "Tell on, tell on!"

Many got up excitedly from their winter quarters and rushed out to new places, as if to help spread the exciting news.

But what the news was, nobody knew.

⤲ SAID BRINK STILLWATER, farmer, looming up out of his newspaper like a bucket of shelled corn set down in the henlot, "First comes the right to know, and then the compulsion to tell somebody."

The Waiting, Little Places

CARL AND MARY Weilhamer were not at home when we got to their Owen County farm, so we waited, although their dog was markedly unenthusiastic about this decision.

They moved to the farm from Indianapolis, where Carl had been a plumber and electrician. He had never even lived on a farm before, but Mary grew up on a farm in Hendricks County. During World War II, Carl was in the Navy, on the *Sacramento*, and Mary was at home with their three children. Carl is big, forthright, and inventive. He likes new people and new adventures. Two of the children are married, and have their own children. One son is in Army service in Vietnam. In this close, loving family, Mary is the clasp on a gold necklace.

From the time we turned off the county road, which is so rough and narrow it seems like somebody's private drive, until we reached the easy-swinging, big farm gate where signs say "Stop" and "Main Street" and "Weilhamer Hills," the farm seemed to say, "This is what I've always wanted to do."

"All my life I've wanted to have a remote place in Indiana where autumn trees are the color of Christmas fire. I will make bird feeders to hang in the yard and will not allow anybody to hunt in the woods.

"I've always wanted to go to farm sales, and know the farmers, and buy obsolete farming implements like walking plows, cultivators, wheat drills, harrows, dairy wagons, buggies, and paint them bright colors and string them along both sides of a driveway from the barn to the house.

"I want a good, new barn where I can have a workshop and Mary can stable her riding horses. They will always have halters on, so she can catch them in the pasture if I'm not there.

"All my life I've wanted a little merry-go-round horse to set in the yard and an iron hitching post with a horsehead on it painted bright green, at the back gate. And rows of buggy wheels set around. I wanted to collect all sizes of old iron kettles to set them around the yard with benches and tables of native sandstone.

"I wanted an old house that I could fix up without destroying its old-time character, a low stone house, with a paved, roofless front porch, and a sheep bell by the door to ring softly in a high wind.

"For the front window I can use those big old plate-glass windows I got while I lived in Indianapolis and knew what was being torn down and where bargains were available. I wanted lots of light in the living room, and comfortable chairs and a cupboard for Mary to keep her old, pretty dishes in. I wanted a fireplace, and a corner where we could set the Christmas tree and decorate it with all the homemade and accumulated ornaments we've used since that Christmas Eve in the Depression when we were married.

"Of course I'd want electricity . . . I could do the wiring myself and save money . . . and a furnace and bathroom. And a radio so I could get the war news while Mike's in Vietnam.

"All my life I've wanted my home road to be a narrow, stony one with a noisy plank bridge to cross and side ditches that run brimful after a heavy summer rain. I wanted one mailbox near the main road, to get my Sunday paper in, and another on the smaller road, near the gate, to get the weekday mail and papers in.

"I wanted a piece of land where spring rains green up the pastures and keep some springs and creeks running the year round. A place where Mary and I can walk, ride horses, or sit and watch the birds and have people come.

"This is it."

⩔ SUMMER IS OVER. This coolness is not summer's after-rain chill, and it is not quite autumn's chill, either.

The lilac bushes have dropped their leaves in a disheveled ring on the ground, like the trimmed-off overhang of pastry dropped onto the board, when you're making a pie.

This is the chill that advises you to discard those plans for things you were going to do this summer and get a good start, now, on what you planned to accomplish last winter.

⩔ "BEAUTY IS IN THE EYE of the beholder," said Margaret Hungerford, accurately, except for the word "eye." Beauty is in the heart of the beholder.

In beautiful Indiana, October is the time when, if you know some brushy, weed-taken little place, off by itself, you should drop everything and go there.

A little patch that was a pasture or cropfield in the era when a small farm could support a family in fair comfort; land overtaken now by sassafras and sumac, tall ironweed and goldenrod waving its un-Midas wand that turns nothing to gold except itself; where dried Queen Anne's lace and faded thistle with the down spilling out of it, and milkweed that has opened its gray-green boats, make protective cover for little accessory plants growing under them.

Places no longer productive of farm crops, but not yet in the clutch of land developers. Ringed by wooded hills and sheltered by a tent of infinite October blue sky, these little places just lie there. Year after year, they just wait. They have their harvest time. It is rich, and it is now. For man's need of land is not only for food and shelter but equally for occasional solitude.

Two such places are near this farm, beside the back road that I take when I have to get a column quickly to the nearest post office. From one the house has vanished from the steep hill, leaving only the roofless springhouse gouged into the side of the hill and the husk of an old barn at the foot of it.

Even the door of the springhouse is gone now, but the walls of thick limestone chunks put together skillfully many years ago are still solid, and long ferns hang down from the earth collected between the stones. Standing on the hillside, you can look over the springhouse wall and see the clear water running across the mud-covered stone floor.

All the buildings are gone from the other waiting, little place, the old "Pa Dutton place" across the road. It belongs to a limestone company. Far back in one of the brushy fields, where some stone was quarried out a long time ago, there is an old grout pile. From the road it looks like ancient Roman ruins.

It is a long time since Pa Dutton farmed here and, in his thrifty Dutch way, made a comfortable living from a difficult farm. His sons, Jim and Emerson, eventually bought good farms in another part of the community.

Pa Dutton's well is still there, deep and cool and dark, its stone wall greened with moss. You can easily recognize the place where the house stood, near it. There were limestone outcroppings on Pa Dutton's farm and the soil was thin. There were teams of work horses to feed and curry, chickens and hogs to be looked after, cows to milk, suppers to be eaten. There were roosters that crowed in the chilly mornings when Jim and Emerson were getting dressed to do the barn chores and eat breakfast before they walked to the one-room school a mile and a half away. They carried their lunches and cut through the fields, crossed a creek and a wood, and came to the Wampler schoolhouse on a hilltop across from the Maple Grove church.

The wilderness simply waited until the boys grew up and left. Then it crept back over Pa Dutton's place. No man ever really owns the land; it belongs to itself and a farmer should regard it with more of humility than a sense of ownership.

In autumn now the hills there are mounds of pink, russet, gold, scarlet, and brown, with enough green left to make the splendor bearable. Every bush and tree in those waiting, little places offers its individual poetry of color and shape.

The reason this land can lie idle, making no income for its owners, and in fact incurring tax expense, is that under its shallow soil, the owners believe, valuable building limestone waits.

In the meantime the two old farms can just lie there "unimproved," holding their "overburden" in prodigal magnificence.

↘ "ROSE COTTAGE" was the real name of the country school Mary Weilhamer went to, near New Winchester in Hendricks County, but everybody called it "Shakerag" because, instead of ringing a bell when recess was over, the teacher came to the door and waved a white handkerchief, Mary said.

"My mother went there," Mary told me. "She was

born in 1881. My father went there, too. And once my older sister tried to teach Shakerag. She had gone one summer to Danville Normal. It was her first school. Some of the children were as old as she was, and some of the boys were bigger. She couldn't keep order. When the bigger boys began climbing out of the windows she gave up the school. She was more successful in another school where she was a stranger to begin with.

"We had good times in that school. Every Friday afternoon we had spelling bees, or programs and recitations. The people of the community came and took part, too. Sometimes we had box suppers at night. I still remember some of the recitations I learned for those Shakerag Friday afternoons. And I can still spell the words, too."

She laughed, then asked, "What is the rest of that poem that begins, 'The year's at the spring'?"

IN SCHOLARLY, old-fashioned writing, Jesse C. Brooks, Henry County farmer, wrote, "It was exactly sixty-nine years ago this fall that I taught my first country school. I have witnessed the asafetida practice. There were a number of children that would pull that little bag up out of their collar bands and suck a few draws to further their chances of immunity to colds, fevers, whooping cough, diphtheria, and such things. I recall, too, that these certain families seldom had any sickness."

At eighty-nine, Mr. Brooks rents out the tillable parts of his farm, but takes care of the hogs himself. This year, from nine brood sows, he raised and fed ninety hogs. He has lived on a farm all his life.

"When I began teaching school," he says, "I had

graduated from high school and taken a short Normal course, and held a teaching license. My salary was forty dollars a month, which included the fee for attending the Saturday Teachers' Institute.

"The school, two miles from Arlington in Rush County, was fourteen miles from my home. I got a boarding place about a mile and a quarter from the school, with a fine young married couple. But I had never been away from home overnight more than two or three times in my life. By the first Wednesday I was the most homesick young man you ever saw.

"The school was a large, one-room building, heated by two wood-burning stoves. The teacher was also the janitor. It was long before the era of school buses; the children walked to school, carrying their lunches, and the teacher did the same."

In his first school were forty-five pupils, of whom six or seven were beginners. "School opened at eight in the morning, closed at four in the afternoon if possible. We had fifteen-minute recitation periods. In reading, spelling, and arithmetic, we often had two classes going at once, some doing work on the blackboard, some orally. Spelling was written on tablet paper, alternately with pronouncing words through assignment. Pupils exchanged and graded the papers."

He remembers it happily. "They were a nice group of country people, well behaved. I never had to use harsh discipline. Had two or three boys that tried chewing tobacco at noon or recess. I taught six years in the common schools and worked up to a salary of sixty dollars a month. Then I married, quit teaching, and went to farming."

🕊 "SHE WROTE POETRY," said Gertie Wenrich, sitting in Dick's big green chair and speaking in her brisk way. "She was an old woman. She had a dishful of poems and made them into a book for me. I love to read them. One was about how lonely she was when she was old. I wish I had known she was so lonely. I would have visited her more often. When you're young yourself you don't realize these things."

Gertie is ninety years old now and is living in a trailer along the Maple Grove road near her married son Cleo. His wife, Lorena, had brought Gertie here that afternoon.

Before all the small country schools of this county were consolidated, Gertie cooked at the school where all the Maple Grove children went. She was an excellent cook and a good friend to the children, knowing all of them and their parents as neighbors.

For the past several years she has divided her time between trailers, one in Cleo's yard, the other in Florida, near her other son, Calvin. She likes living in trailers. "But I didn't like Martha's trailer," she said fiercely, "it's too little. In my trailer I have room for everything I want and need to do." Gertie is little and lighthearted. With her sitting in Dick's big chair, the chair looked almost as big as a trailer, I thought.

While she and Lorena were still here another friend stopped, bringing her mother, Sally Sargeant, who also is ninety years old. The two ninety-year-olds were like two little girls who have each accompanied a mother on a social call and are getting acquainted. Each at once wrote down the date of the other's birthday and promised to send a card. They could have had a delightful little tea party without any of the rest of us, if I had brought out a set of doll dishes and some water.

Mrs. Sargeant has large, dark eyes that lighted up as she talked. She smiles most of the time whether talking or listening. She used to play the organ at a country church and, when asked, got up and played some hymns on the piano for us. She sews, and had made the smartly tailored dress she was wearing.

"My husband was one of the three first rural mail carriers back in 1905," she said. He was a farmer. She still has a home on five acres of the farm, which is near Burns City. She lives there in good weather and spends the winters with one or another of her six children.

Asked if her husband drove the old-time enclosed-cab buggy for delivering mail, she laughed and said, "Oh, my goodness, no! There weren't any roads then. He rode a horse."

She remembered many of the old-time crafts which in their day were more necessary than charming. She remembered her mother canning fruit in stone jars and pouring melted sealing wax, hot and odorous, around the rim to hold the stone lid in place. "The foods didn't keep well," she added. "People dried corn and fruits a good deal. Later they had glass jars."

She remembered making soap. Made with lye it was white, but made with leachings from ashes it was dark and never got really firm. She remembered smoking meat; they hung the joints in a smokehouse over a low fire of hickory wood and corncobs burning in a big iron kettle, she said. They made apple butter in a big kettle, too.

She remembered picking geese to make feather beds and pillows. "You held their heads between your knees and their feet in one hand, and plucked the down with the other hand," she explained, gesturing to show how it was. "The geese squawked. I felt sorry for them. They were fat and sometimes little patches of fat came out with the feathers, on the ends."

She was like a charming little volume of history, well read and cherished.

Ψ FROM OUTSIDE, Mr. Coffman's yard looked like the place where old washing machines, refrigerators, and gas stoves go when they die if they have been good. But there was a Tennessee farm wagon in front of the shop, in good condition, with spring seat, faded green bed, muddy red front wheels, and that was why Dick had wanted to come back from Scottsburg by way of those narrow, crooked roads that had more one-way bridges than I would have guessed were left in Indiana.

While he examined the wagon I went into the shop. It was not a place of antiques, or of junk, either. It was more just miscellany. Miscellany was displayed from shelves, lined up in orderly fashion on the floor, piled in bins, hung against walls. There was a bin of old books, mostly grammars and spellers. I spent some time looking at these before I even saw the bin of dirty, oil-darkened old wooden shoe forms.

They were hand-carved. They had square toes because they were made in an era when shoes were square-toed, long before the present popular return. I picked up one form that was the size of the very modern squared-toed shoe my sister Nina wears now. It was pretty and graceful, reminded me joyously of her foot and I bought it. Immediately all those old shoe forms began to remind me of the feet of people I know. What possession is, anyway, more individually expressive than a person's everyday shoe?

There were forms for making men's shoes, and women's. Some very small ones could have been for children's shoes or women with very small feet. Some had detachable wooden instep pieces by which a form could be adjusted to model boot, shoe, or slipper as the cobbler required. The underside, delicately carved to fit close to the arch, was almost as expressive as a real foot, and the many tack holes in them showed they had been used over and over. Even more poignant were the alterations that had been made, to accommodate an individual foot, the tackings of little pieces of leather for a shoe that had to make way for a bunion, or a misshapen toe.

One pair, long, slim, and pale, suggested youthful, gaily walking feet and these reminded me of the farm daughter, so I bought them for her. When I got them back to the farm they reminded me so vividly of her it was a long time before I could bear to send them away from the farm.

The oily dust came off onto my hands as I went over every one of the eloquent old lasts in that bin. It was almost like reading a Spoon River anthology. "Shorty" Coffman and Dick came in when they had finished the sale of the wagon. I was still handling the shoe forms.

"Now you wash those and they'll come out just as clean and pretty," suggested Shorty. "They're hard maple."

I asked about the cobbler who had used them.

"Dan Perrin," said Shorty. "He came from Kentucky. You can ask anybody in Jackson County about Dan. Everybody remembers him."

Shorty knew him well. It was in fact he who had found the cobbler dead in the shoeshop two years earlier.

"He was a little, short, fat man and had a funny, curling-up kind of mustache," said Shorty's wife. "He took short, quick steps when he walked."

Dan was ninety-three years old when he died. He had been a cobbler in Brownstown sixty-five years and his father was a cobbler there before he became one. "He made harness, too, and wove cane seats in chairs. He worked day and night," said Shorty. "His wife was an Indian woman from out West someplace. She had very black hair and always wore it parted in the middle and hanging straight down."

"It never turned gray at all," said Mrs. Coffman. "She wore peculiar shoes. Dan made a plaster cast of her foot so he could make special shoes for her. I wonder what ever became of that cast? It was around here a long time."

The cobbler was an impatient man. Shorty had warned him not to try to move the shoe machine by himself. "I told him I'd come and help him, but he couldn't wait. He tried to move it by himself and it toppled over on him. He was dead when I found him in his shop the next morning."

🔽 "THE BEST THING a farmer gets on a long vacation away from home," said Brink Stillwater, who never takes a long vacation, "is homesick."

A Columnist's Hazards

ONCE ON THE ROAD to the Weilhamer place we saw reindeer moss growing, a magical-looking, blue-green lichen that grows well on that meager, yellow sandstone topsoil, but if you set a clump of it onto a more fertile soil someplace else, it dies.

Trees in the woods there have made a dense cover,

but never grew very tall. Beside the narrow road we found the tall, three-pronged tickle grass that is a pioneer in shallow soil, and pussytoes that can survive drought.

Even houses are sparse along that part of the road. As we crossed a little bridge where a creek ran at the foot of a steep hill, I looked up and shivered at the dramatically bleak, little faded brown house perched on the top of the hill, like an empty book. There was a new driveway leading up to it.

Mary said, "It's been sold to a young man from the city who likes to come out for recreation on weekends. We knew the old man who lived there. We visited him often. We liked him. He said he saw spirits. They were white, he said, and came to the creek at the foot of the hill. On summer nights he played his guitar for them and they danced. They were good spirits, kind, he said. Sometimes they came into his house and he played for them there.

"He had cataracts on his eyes and I've been told people with cataracts see streaks of light . . . that may be what he thought were spirits. When he moved his head . . . as he played the guitar, you know . . . they would move, too."

Maybe. Probably. But, going home, when we came to the place of the reindeer moss, two beautiful pale-brown deer leaped out of the road. From noplace, and disappeared into the woods, just like magic, like spirits.

⍋ "It's so quiet and peaceful here," wistfully murmured Carl Frye, who was the high-school band director when the farm's son and daughter played in the band. His wife, Martha, had brought a book of thank-you let-

174

ters from her kindergarten class, which had visited the farm a few days earlier.

It was near dusk of an early-summer day, warm enough to be comfortable without a sweater. The yard smelled of fresh-cut grass, Ma Nees's old-fashioned moss rose was showing its first pink buds, sweet rockets were purple splashes in the raspberry patch, where they shouldn't have been. In the strawberry patch, recently rescued from grass and weeds, strawberries were reddening. Ducks, geese, and Bantams were going quietly about their evening affairs, and out in the green pasture east of the barn the cattle were grazing comfortably, switching their tails. The farm did seem quiet and peaceful just then. Yet every inch was being competed for by more plant life than it could possibly support. The driveway, where Carl was standing, was pale brown from maple seeds whirled down out of the trees. Even so only a small part of the year's crop had fallen and deep in the heart of every seed was the hope of another tree.

In the owl box the baby screech owl waited for darkness to gather so the parents could catch him a supper of some creature likewise out hunting supper. That night a raccoon raided the duck's nest in the machinery shed, taking all but three of her pale-green eggs, and cleaned out another nest near there on a bale of hay. Some nocturnal creature, more hungry than afraid of the angry, hissing goose there, took nearly all of the eggs she had been brooding for nearly a month.

So what are the components of peace and quiet? Speak to the earth and it will teach you about the laws of hunger and predation, symbiosis, death, birth, and the ways of keeping the balance. Earth will teach you about sustaining life and evolving new forms.

In the natural world quiet is not always peace. It may mean merely a stomach temporarily satisfied, or fatigue, or fear. It may even mean defeat or resignation.

Peace is an accessory to a situation, not a thing of itself.

Predation is an essential step in nature's great chain of life, and peace occurs at a point of balance between predation and survival. But the aspect of peace and quiet that Carl Frye sensed on the farm that evening is genuine. It is one of the farm's indigenous characteristics.

IN COMPARISON to a city, a farm is a quiet place, and if you listen to the quietness, as you would examine a piece of moss under a microscope, you can identify the separate components. This winter morning the quietness is dominated by the sound of wind. In the driveway a long, dead maple limb drops with a heavy sigh and breaks into three pieces. At the breaks you can see holes pecked into the dead wood by birds seeking the insects that had caused the limb to die.

In the lilac bush a small rusty cowbell chatters, but the heavy iron dinner bell on its post nearby says nothing. The bell rope swings gently, so frayed it would break if anything stronger than wind pulled it.

Softly sorrowing, Zorba, the black bull, walks along the woven wire fence in the springlot. A singing chickadee adds several extra "dees" to its longest song, and the separate notes fall down through the morning air like ripe fruits dropping. A neighbor's red car swishes past on the way to a town job and the neighbor waves. From rain-soaked pastures behind the barn comes the mallard's psalm of thankfulness for small new rivers and lakes created by last night's rain, and the pond level raised almost to the red clay brim.

This morning a neighbor is brush-hogging a corner of his field near our boundary line and the sound reaches faintly into the farmhouse.

These sounds are the ingredients of farm quiet; they blend well and thereby produce a unified quietness.

⟱ ONE MAY MORNING the lilacs were in full bloom, in strutted peaks like a cow's udder when milking has been too long delayed. That morning on an errand that took me past the lilac bushes, I pulled down a splendid seven-pronged cluster and took time to appreciate its depth of fragrance. It was just after a rain, the time when lilacs are at their finest. Rain brings out the whole fragrant eloquence.

Good thing I took the time that day. Only a few days later the lilacs were merely drying, brown memories. Jonquils, narcissus, hyacinths, went the same hurried pace. Violets, redbud, and dogwood, in their respective hours, lingered only a little longer.

⟱ MY SISTER NINA once told me, "The trouble with columnists is after a few years they tend to pontificate."

It has been several years now since I began writing a column from this farm for newspapers in Indianapolis and Muncie, and heaven preserve me from pontificating. As Sylvia Cordwood said, "My opinion is something that is true for me. My conviction is something that is true for everybody . . . in my opinion."

The surest way to avoid pontificating, of course, is

to stop writing. Next best is to adopt a new writing form, say, poetry.

In my several years of writing a farm column I have had many letters from which I realize people instinctively turn to poetry to express their thoughts about "nature." Many unpublished poets have sent me their little mimeographed books. It isn't always good poetry, but it is good therapy, and it is sincere, and when you know the story you appreciate both the poem and the poet.

🌱 "LET ME SHOW YOU my anthology," Dick said, taking out his billfold. By the time he had drawn out the snapshots and school pictures of the farm son and daughter and the more recent ones of their daughters, Suzannah Mason and Rachel Jane, those words had become a poem.

Poetry, being imaginative, fresh, and honest, is the very language of children, and in a family many of their incidental remarks are, essentially, love poems.

Once when we were in the living room with a guest, Carol came and sat close to me on the sofa and whispered, "Will you look at me, too, some of the times, and smile, and speak to me?" This is one version of the eternal child's eternal love poem to its world.

One year for her Christmas shopping she had fifty cents and was about to spend it all on something for me. Dick, helping her shop, told her not to "shoot the whole wad on one person." She said, "But, Dick, I love her that much!" It became a family proverb, but to me it was an enduring love poem.

A Columnist's Hazards

↯ EVEN BEFORE THE PONTIFICATOR began writing a column, he should have had some practice in writing poetry. It is the very best of writing discipline, requiring brevity, and a habit of taking a fresh, imaginative look at familiar things. It can be intensely frank without giving its author the feeling of being naked in public because it expresses personal feelings in a code that makes them seem universal. This, perhaps, is why after writing several books of poetic prose, anthropologist Loren Eiseley published the poems he had been secretly taking refuge in from boyhood on.

The pontificating columnist, struggling to cut down five pages of vital notes into a page and a half and still present his story, will appreciate his previous struggles for brevity, in his poetry practice. By the same reasoning, the irritated reader of a labyrinthine government bulletin is likely to wish all government reports had to be written in poetry.

If a pontificator has to have a practical reason for writing poetry, there are some; for one thing, in this tension-prone society it is a better sleep inducer than counting sheep. And it is prophetic, with a thought to the future. In the progress of the world toward its ultimate reshaping, poets and comic-book writers have always been first to believe in the impossible and make it quotable.

A poet is therefore a prophet, and a pontiff was a kind of priest. It was a poet, Dr. Earl Marlatt, teacher, theologian, writer, traveler, Army officer, friend of youth, and Indiana's poet laureate, who summed it up. He said, "It is the duty of priests and poets of all ages to keep the faith-fires burning." That, of course, includes a niche for the pontificators.

When I first met Grace Mitchell she was a retired librarian and giving away books. She lived in a house that had books stored in banana crates in the attic. It was her house, inherited from her schoolteaching Aunt Clara Murphy, with whom she had lived when she was studying library science and afterward when she was a librarian. Aunt Clara had stored the books in the attic; many of them were Greek, Latin, and English-literature textbooks.

In her librarian years Grace had been too busy to do anything with them, but now, "going through everything," she was giving them away. It was from her I got my treasured copy of *John Plowman's Talk*, which sits on the shelf beside *The Prose of John Clare* and Alan Moorehead's *Darwin and the Beagle*.

"Is there some special preservative in banana crates?" I asked, sitting across from the librarian at a dinner given by her cousin Helen Stewart. "Russell Ranard told me that a banana stalk hung in the henhouse will get rid of mites. I tried it and it works."

Grace laughed. "Well, the books kept all right," she agreed. She has fine, short-cut white hair and blue eyes that see everything. That day she was wearing a pink sweater. "When I was a child," she said, "I always wanted to wear pink or red and couldn't because my hair was red."

In the third grade in the Mitchell public school she had sat in front of Bob Collins, who, many years later when they were about to be married, told her he had always wanted to dip the end of one of those long red braids into his inkwell.

In her younger days, Grace said she was self-conscious about being left-handed because "I thought it made me seem different from other people." At the table, four other guests were left-handed. "I never thought anything about it," said Iris, whose handwriting in no way resembles the usual back-slanted left-hand script.

Even before she retired and had time for it, Grace had gone into research of her family genealogy, always searching for cousins. She was always telling me about cousins, finding new ones, meeting others wherever I went with her, and looking up more that she knew only by hearsay. She was, somehow, a cousin of my neighbor Iris and her sister Helen, and it was in honor of a mutual cousin, visiting from California, that Helen had given the dinner.

I understood this research better after Grace and I went to a festival together someplace and on the way home she said, "I never really had a normal family life, with brothers and sisters and parents. I always lived with a grandmother, or an aunt." But she had many friends and knew someone wherever she went.

Even while she was giving away Aunt Clara's books, she was collecting others, especially cookbooks. She never did much cooking, partly because she was living alone, but also because "Aunt Edith and Aunt Clara were both excellent cooks and I always felt the best way I could help was to stay out of their way in the kitchen." Now she had joined a cookbook club. "Not to cook out of. To read," she explained. "They make wonderful reading, you know."

She told us the recipe of a casserole she thought sounded good, which she had just heard about. "You begin by smashing up some shredded wheat. And then you pour shrimp soup over it. I'd use mushroom soup instead, I think. I don't care much for shrimp and such things."

She may have changed her food tastes by now, though, and learned to enjoy shrimp. Because a few years after she retired she went on a vacation and again met Bob. By that time he was seventy-six, a widower, a grandfather, an excellent cook, and retired from years of being a "government revenooer."

He lived in a trailer in California and when Grace married him she sold her house, disposed of most of the furniture, and became a total book uncollector. And probably acquired a lot of cousins.

🐦 AFTER LIVING TWO WEEKS in a house whereof the porch, my writing place, is being rebuilt because termites have finally eaten through to its old bones, thus disproving the saying that termites will not eat yellow poplar, my soul yearns after the tidy places I have known.

I remember my long-ago farm neighbor Rennie Dutton, whose house was immaculate even in housecleaning time. Rennie made the best doughnuts in the world, a big milk-crockful at a cooking, and when I walked down to her house, taking along our companionable German shepherd dog, Bishop, she fed him fresh doughnuts, too.

I think of the utterly clean-looking hayfield, after the hay has been mowed, raked, baled, and removed before it gets rained on, and of a golden ripe wheatfield with bobwhites singing about it nearby.

I think of a dove and how gracefully her classic profile curves along the smooth-feathered head and back, giving her such a look of harmony that a dove has become the symbol of peace and the shape of it would mean peace if you discovered it in the script of any language. Then I remember the dove's sloppily flung-together nest on a low limb of the maple tree and how she quarrels with her mate, and I wonder whether peace is really order and harmony, or just an interval in which nothing is happening.

I think of the pale-green lining of a pea pod, freshly picked and opened, and of the green freshness of peas just shelled out of it and indented slightly from having been pressed close together in the pod. I think of the immaculate, tiny tile shapes making a pattern on an ear of sweet corn where the yellow and white grains have been cut off in slabs, being prepared for canning or freezing. I remember the masses of creamy-white elderberry bloom rising in delicate fragrance from the green, weedy bank beside an abandoned old railroad bed I know of beside the road to Ellettsville.

I think of the clean, coppery youngness of baby Duroc pigs; of the glossy black and white fur of the cat Witchy, who spends half her time licking that fur. I remember the oriole's nest, fallen from its lofty place in the maple tree, after two years of sheltering baby orioles. It was rain-washed and gray and had side tabs woven over the tree limb to hold it in place and it hung high over the driveway. It was a deep, pliant cradle, woven of delicate fibers of bark and firm, fine grasses, green when just finished, turning gray as it aged.

I think of the rain-washed, wind-rubbed walls of an old poplar barn from which all the paint is long gone if ever there was any paint on it. It is the cleanest gray I know. I think how it collects the warmth of early-spring sunlight and deflects it back onto the grateful, shaggy bodies of cattle standing near. And while I think of this I shiver and wait for the carpenters to come back and finish the back porch so I can restore order there and move in again, with the typewriter.

⚹ "ANYTHING YOU LIKE to do you can make a success of," said eighty-five-year-old Piney Brewer, who has made a marked success of raising cattle, and no success at all of keeping her house empty.

In the Gosport telephone directory she is listed as Pauline, but townspeople call her Piney. Her real name, as she pronounces it, is Paliney Jane. She was named for two aunts.

Her grandfather, a professor, was an Irishman and came to America to survey a railroad and got here in time to vote for Abraham Lincoln for President. When Piney's father moved his family from Jordan Village to Gosport, where Piney and her nine brothers and sisters grew up, her mother thought they were leaving Paradise.

But Piney thinks there are no better people in the world than those around Gosport, or Paragon, or Owen or Morgan County, in all of which places the now wealthy, unspendthrift cattlewoman owns land. She has a high opinion of the commission house to which she has sent cattle since 1935, and although she quarrels with him she has high regard for the trucker who hauls for her.

She was not really poor when she went into the cattle business but she says, "I had to do it alone." She had a feed store. Her brother Gar was running a grist mill which burned a few years after his death in 1950.

Her sister Mame, who drove the car and kept the house, cared nothing for cattle and tried to discourage Piney from raising them. Piney cared nothing for housekeeping and never learned to drive a car.

At a neighbor's dispersal sale she bought four Shorthorn cows, including Dad's Girl, which the neighbor told her privately was his best cow. She paid sixteen dollars for each cow, borrowed a neighbor's bull, and now has six of her own for her herd, which is Hereford instead of Shorthorn.

Dad's Girl was the start of a herd that eventually numbered three hundred cows. At one low-ebb time Piney sold calves for three dollars each. One year, from seventy-nine cows she sold seventy-eight calves. "I got so I could do my own veterinary work," she boasted modestly, "even deliver a calf when the cow needed help. Mame always said, 'One of these days a cow will kick you into the next world,' but none ever did."

Piney is not a large woman. At eighty-five she is still attractive enough that you can understand why in high school she was voted the prettiest girl in her class. "I never went to see a doctor in my life nor had one come to see me," she told me.

As her cattle herd increased, she also increased her landholdings and now owns around a thousand acres. She has "some odd pieces" east of the railroad in Gosport, some "low bottom" between Gosport and Romona, some more in Owen County, where giant foxtail has the farm by the throat, and two hundred acres in Morgan County, where she has an excellent tenant and sends a hundred cows every year for wintering. That farm has "a hundred acres of good corn, green pasture, lots of good baled hay, an electric pump that brings up river water at the push of a button." She has a good, strong voice, lives alone in a big, unkempt house, and likes to talk over the phone.

"It's a miracle what you can do with cattle," she told me earnestly, "but it takes practically all of your time."

ᘺ   "WE'RE FILLING THE SILO this week," Iris said, "and the green beans are ready. I want to get them all picked so I can dust the vines. Besides I want you to have all you can use." So an hour before time to start dinner I took baskets and went down. Iris's kitchen was filled with the good smell of beef and potatoes and onions cooking, and she was baking a pie. She has two cookstoves in the kitchen. One burns bottled gas, the other burns wood or coal. She was cooking on the gas stove. A peck basket of freshly gathered tomatoes was on a corner of the long table in the middle of the room and two split-hickory chairs were drawn up to the table. Through the glass doors of a china cabinet you can see Iris's best dishes, and the carnival glass dish the teacher gave her in the second grade, and her grandmother's old glass bread plate.

Iris went out to the garden with me, but couldn't stay on account of the pie. We went past a row of typical farm garden flowers, yellow marigolds, blue cornflowers, zinnias of many colors, tall yellow gladioli and some of a burning scarlet. Green beans were hanging abundantly from nine-foot-tall tepees in a long row.

From five tepees I filled two bushel baskets, then marked the stopping place by a stick in the ground, and went in to tell Iris goodbye. Carr had come in for dinner and showed me the new saddle his son George had bought.

George lives in town, keeps horses at the farm, and his children come there to ride. It was a handsome saddle, black leather with embossed silver ornaments on the martingales and hooded stirrups, and a red-leather seat.

I promised to bake Iris two lemon pies for her silo dinner and she gave me two oversized cucumbers. "Have you ever cooked cucumbers as you cook eggplant? You split them lengthwise, let them stand in salt water as you do eggplant. Roll them in flour or cracker crumbs and fry them. They have their own individual flavor and we like it better than eggplant."

There was just time, I thought, to try it for dinner. In farmhouses, dinner is at noon.

↘ FAY AND JULIE HANCOCK have been married sixty years and are still such good friends that Fay frames Julie's button collections and at an auction recently paid $4.50 for another toothpick holder for her collection that has already spread over the end of the dining room like ivy across an old church wall. And Julie willingly gave up the whole basement to the fifty-two miniatures Fay has made, duplicating horse-drawn vehicles and farm implements he remembers from boyhood and early farm life.

On the Sunday when Fay and Julie celebrated their sixtieth wedding anniversary, guests spent a good deal of time in the basement.

Julie might be partial to the red-upholstered buggy with the red frame and rolled-up top because "it's just like the one I courted her in sixty-one years ago," Fay said. He is partial to several. One is "Old Balim," an old

Negro man driving a donkey to a buggy. "That's old Balim," Fay said. "He was a real person. He always followed the circus parade with his donkey and an old buggy filled with young boys. And I was one of the boys." He likes the sod plow, with a small boy riding the horse to guide it while a man holds the plow in the stubborn ground. Fay was that boy, too. He spent seventeen years in Dakota using a sod plow. He likes the chilled Oliver plow like the one he used first, when he was eleven years old.

Or the stone-filled wagon pulled by a work team. "I made my living with horses, and farming," Fay said. "When Julie and I were first married I hauled stone in a wagon like that for the roads in Illinois. A yard and a half was a wagonload."

He liked the utterly equipped huckster wagon, replica of "Dolph Cooter's huckster wagon" that carried a complete line of merchandise and a sign that offered to get anything you wanted and didn't see. It has groceries, pans and kettles, farming tools, paintings, and ginseng. Chickens taken in trade ride in the coop under the wagon body. Tacked to the sides are miniature furs made of pieces of real fur . . . mink, rabbit, raccoon, possum. Behind the huckster's wagon two customers are waiting, a long-skirted mother and an eager small boy who is looking for "that striped stick of candy that was so good," Fay says.

He finds his materials in all kinds of unexpected places; all kinds of odd things suggest use as some part of a horse-drawn miniature. An odd-shaped ceramic planter, with a top added, became a stagecoach. For another stagecoach with a ready-made Italian body he had to pay fifteen dollars, but he couldn't resist it. A stick of red cedar Carr gave him last winter became a bobsled like one Carr used to pull with a team of big Percherons, Pat and Mike. Other miniatures, all expressive of some interest or experience dear to Fay's heart, are a Greek cart with green horses; a Roman racing chariot with a body made of a Crisco can and decorations cut from a fancy leather belt; a team pulling a wagon through a vine-draped covered bridge; a log wagon with three real beech logs chained onto it; a "Tennessee team," horse and mule hitched together; a doctor's buggy pulled by a tired old white horse and going to see a patient late at night; a dairy wagon; a balky horse being backed up to a railway-express loading platform; a rural mail carrier's buggy; two covered wagons; a working team with the colt tied to the mare's side; a fringe-topped surrey; a buckboard; and many old-time implements.

Some take a long time to make; the eight-horse beer wagon took three years. Fay had to have hickory barrels specially cut. Julie helped him fasten the bark hoops on them. Fay dresses the dolls. "I would use more drivers," Fay explained, "but it's hard to find man dolls." Some miniatures include dogs. One is a farm scene that includes poultry, cattle, horses, sheep, a little creek made of a mirror, a water gap that opens, and a bridge over the creek. "Took me a long time to assemble all those things," Fay said. "I'm real proud of it."

In 1928 he was chief of police in the county seat, but has not yet made a horse-drawn vehicle to commemorate it. Later he became an auctioneer. His son followed him into the profession after graduating from the university. Fay's daughter Lois, a teacher and influenced by his miniatures perhaps, collects old-time farming tools, house accessories, and implements.

For Fay, the basement is a book, his own autobiography.

⩔ "I LIKE ELVON," said Brink Stillwater, farmer. "The only way I'd fault him is, he's impractical. He wants to eat his cake and keep yours."

A Cake Not Turned

🐦 AT SUPPERTIME of a bitterly cold February evening Dick came down to the house pushing a wheelbarrow. On a bed of straw in it was a black calf that looked like a dead or dying dog. "I was just starting down to supper," Dick said, "and I saw a little black leg stickin' out from behind that old fanning mill in the front corner of the barn."

The calf was two days old. Born to an inexperienced mother, she had somehow managed to slide under the slatted gate of the stall before she got the first vital pull of milk, and in her effort to stand, had got down to the cold concrete floor where Dick found her.

Waves of cold air rose from her black coat and she shivered violently. We pushed the wheelbarrow close to the wall and put a heating pad on her. Her eyes rolled back and she stretched out her neck as if to die.

After half an hour we pried open her cold mouth and poured in a small amount of warm milk. After a long while she twitched one ear slightly.

Later we left her in the wheelbarrow while we watched a TV show of the assassination of Abraham Lincoln. Just as John Wilkes Booth leaped onto the stage, the calf upset the wheelbarrow with a pistol-loud clatter. She had stopped shivering now and wanted to explore the kitchen. We gave her another drink of milk.

At bedtime Dick put a big wooden box in the bedroom, ringed it about with kitchen chairs, and the calf spent the night there. She bawled only once, and then very softly. By morning her coat was normally warm and Dick took her back to the cow. The mother was not hostile, but had no idea why the calf was there, and the calf, now believing food comes from a bottle with a sheep's nipple on it, had no idea how useful the cow could be.

Within a few days, however, they had been re-educated and the calf was as frisky as if she had not escaped from the icy rim of death. She became a pet, useful when schoolchildren visited the farm that spring.

A Cake Not Turned

☙ MY SISTER NINA, who loves "all creatures great and small," lives in a large city. She came to the farm one May morning after a cold, hard rain, the kind farmers call "a toad strangler" or "a goose drownder." By afternoon the sun came out, the wet fields sparkled greenly, and we went up into the pasture to see the new colt. He stopped his playing long enough to kick the mare in the flank. She continued placidly grazing, keeping a watchfulness around him like an invisible fence. Life on the farm seemed, just then, tender, protected.

Stooping to come under the barbed-wire fence, we saw a featherless baby bird lying on the rain-beaten ground. There was not even a blade of grass there for a cushion. The naked, bony body, in its transparent yellow skin, looked like some prehistoric creature. While we were pitying it, the stubby, featherless wings moved just enough to show that the will to live still flickered there. We brought it to the kitchen and covered it so it could die in comfort.

At bedtime I heard a soft, insistent chirping and when I lifted back the cover the bird opened a huge, yellow-rimmed mouth. Its tongue moved, the bony head wobbled from the effort of holding open a cavernous, square mouth. Swatches of yellow down, now dry, stood up on the back and skull.

I went out to the garden to dig worms and, while digging, debated. From the bird's viewpoint it was an act of mercy. From the worm's viewpoint, the worm already in good health and performing a useful service to the soil, it might be an act of betrayal. Especially since the bird might die even after eating the worm.

Nevertheless, when the bird opened its cave, I put one moist, pink end of worm into it. Convulsions of swallowing followed. One unswallowed end of worm dangled, struggling, outside of the yellow rim while the other end was visible through the transparent skin as it went down the throat.

Eventually I substituted bread soaked in milk and later bits of hamburger. Even so, it was necessary sometimes to give water from a spoon to assist the swallowing. For every portion swallowed, an equal amount of black and white semi-fluid was ejected. Parent birds carry this away in their beaks. I shook it onto the ground. On the fifth day the bird was too weak to swallow anything and at midmorning it died. I wrapped it in a red paper napkin and buried it where the farm children always buried their pets and the pitied wild creatures found dead.

There is something in human nature that compels us to interfere in behalf of whatever creature seems in danger of losing the fight. Perhaps this is the measure of man's present divinity.

⚑ THE EFFORT A FARMER MAKES to understand his domestic animals and the wild ones that share his farm keeps his sense of wonder fresh, like the slice of raw apple in the brown sugar jar to keep the sugar from getting hard.

⚑ THE NARROW CRAWLSPACE under this cellarless old house has been a refuge for dogs and cats and many other wild creatures. It was there Rose had her first pups, on a school morning, and at breakfast the unmistakable sound of puppy whimpers came up through the floor, delighting the children but not delighting Dick. In the cold days last winter a possum began coming close to the kitchen door, in daytime. Probably too hungry to be afraid. Or perhaps, possums being nearsighted, the narrow, bright, vertically set eyes did not know it was being watched. Wind blew across the eighteen-inch-long body, parting the coarse black and white hair. The bare tail, dragged along the ground, was the color of an old muddy bone. The pink snout tapered as if sharpened in a giant pencil sharpener, and the black ears were slightly gathered into fullness where they joined the head. The possum walked in a circle holding its head close to the ground, and thus returned finally to the starting point, where it saw and ate the grain of corn it had overlooked at first.

When I slid the door open gently it was gone, instantly, and out of sight beyond the woodpile. After a few days, however, it was tame enough to accept the chunks of doughnut I tossed out. It stood on its hind feet, holding the doughnut between the cold-looking toes of its two front feet, and pulled off bites, tossing them as a dog does, with the lower jaw. Sharp white teeth showed between the drawn-back lips as it ate and I knew they could bite into a small live chick just as easily as into a doughnut. A farmer's concern for his domestic animals collides with the laws of the natural world.

A few weeks later Dick and I looked through the back-room window and watched a possum gathering leaves. She was standing at the garden fenceline, where wind had collected leaves into a deep ridge. With her front feet she scratched them back under her body and onto the prehensile bare tail, packing them firmly with her back feet. When she had enough for a load, she curled the tail tightly around them, like a twine string around newspapers for recycling, and went under the house with her load.

She was obviously preparing a nest. We remembered a possum that had gone into the duck's house one night last spring, when a Bantam was brooding a nest of eggs there, eaten the eggs, frightened the little Bantam up onto a rafter, and then had lain down and gone to sleep in the nest.

Nevertheless, the house-building possum wakened our sympathy. Once you persuade a wild creature to accept food or shelter from you it has tamed you. Now the possum did not seem alien, ugly, or uncouth. She began to seem charming and I hoped to see her children.

There could be as many as fourteen naked marsupials in the pouch, each unshakably attached to a teat. Not all could hope to survive. By the time their nakedness was covered with soft gray fur probably only nine, at most, would be left.

Perhaps the home builder had other ideas. We never saw her emerge with her young.

A long time later, however, a mother possum got into the trap at the barn one night. The trap captures, but does not injure. When we found her, she hissed and showed her small white teeth. I went to bring her some food and water, and when I came back, discovered her pouch was full of gray-furred, rat-sized, squirming possums. Their white, piglike heads looked oversized for the bodies. Their bare tails were pink on the end, their feet were pink and shaped like small bony hands.

For a few weeks we kept them in the poultry battery and fed the mother . . . eggs, chunks of cheese, pieces of cooked or raw chicken, dog food, and apples. She became tame enough to take food out of Dick's hands, and although she always opened her mouth and showed her teeth when people came near her, she was not really afraid or hostile. When she ate an egg she took it between her jaws, then paused as if thinking or getting ready for a shock, or perhaps letting the egg get warm. As she bit into it, the shell snapped with a sharp click and she at once set it on the floor and daintily licked out the contents without spilling any. She used her front feet like hands, and when I saw her raise her pink, bony hands to her face, she seemed almost like a neighbor. I am sure she enjoyed the easy food and the opportunity to rest without fear. But the young possums grew fast and in the closeness of the battery began biting each other's tails. So one night we left the cell door open. The mother was gone the next morning and within twenty-four hours all the young possums left, too.

❄ THERE ARE TWO KINDS of poverty, the proud and the abject. Both wear rags, but with a difference. Proud poverty wears rags elegantly. Abject poverty merges into its rags as if it belonged there.

Trying to alleviate abject poverty is like trying to sew a patch onto a garment of which the fabric is already too weak to hold together under the pressure of needle and thread.

❄ RAIN IN THE NIGHT is saturated with the character of the day just ended. If the day was disappointing or painful, the rain has an overwhelming sound of sadness, anger, or despair. If it was a joyous day, one of promise or achievement, the beginning drops of rain have the sound of applause.

Last night's rain was one that comes only once a year, and it is not even every year one has the pleasure of watching the greening rain, step by step. It was almost like examining a bird's narrow feather under a microscope.

Waking at midnight, I was aware of an unaccustomed light recurring in the southeast, and its answer from the other side of the sky. I got up to look at it. The light came at intervals of about three minutes. Could it be a neighbor's house burning, or cars coming downhill from the church? Could it even be the pilot light in the gas heater doing an unaccustomed and unnecessary ballet? Surely, in winter, it couldn't be lightning.

But it was. A low-placed, orange-red streak like a last shred of sunset was answered by a yellow-bright, high-placed diffusion on the opposite side of the sky. While I went from window to window, marveling, the light increased and thunder began, gently rolling. A white area in the sky just behind the big maple grew and overtook the whole sky, and suddenly the rain began. For ten minutes it fell fast, obscuring the earth, then slowed and fell steadily.

The continuing lightning would release nitrogen into the air and the rain would wash it down to the waiting roots, and by morning the farmscape would be markedly more green.

🐦 FROM SOMEPLACE back of the barn the sorrel mare nickered. Imperatively and several times, as if annoyed or troubled about something. Maybe the colt was caught in the fence, I thought, or being threatened by one of the mules.

Whatever the trouble had been, it was resolved by the time I arrived, hurrying around the corner of the barn. I was just in time to see the mare and colt run across the pasture, the very summation of grace and freedom.

The mare was obviously teaching the colt something. She ran touching him, tossing her head, her mane flowing. The colt ran beside her, equally graceful and swift. Young and full of the joy of motion. He is long-legged. His tail is shorter than the mare's, lacking as yet its full brush. His little pointed ears seemed listening respectfully to every word she said. His charming little fat hips inspired in me a desire to slap them lightly.

Their flight across the pasture was an exercise of pure grace, like the loops and circles in old-time elegant penmanship; like a bird, soaring high above the farmscape; like the curling tendrils of a grapevine. A joy to see.

❧ IN THE HUMAN WORLD there are the bayleaf people, and the parsley people, and what determines who shall be which?

Bayleaf is necessary to things like boiled beef and creole cabbage. It goes in at the start of the cooking and gives its essence to impart distinction to the food. When the food is ready to go to the table, the bayleaf is removed and thrown away.

Parsley, on the other hand, greenly decorative, is laid on the platter for pure glory, and at the last moment, and goes to the table.

IN THE AFTERNOON, having been too long desk-bound, I escaped to the strawberry patch, which fortunately was in need of weeding.

On my desk I left a letter from a man who has made a distinguished career in the city but has not yet forgotten his Indiana farm boyhood experiences.

He had written, "It is possible that like the great reptiles we develop evolutionary characteristics that are self-destructive. I believe we are a part of nature. I do not believe we have any purpose other than that which through our consciousness we create for ourselves. I am not dismayed by the possibility that in two or three billion years the fate of our sun is probably an atomic explosion that will simply volatilize the planets.

"Among the concomitants of consciousness is the ability to notice choices. From this ability, values arise. Bad choices make bad values. I believe that man, through his consciousness, can conceive of the absolute without attaining it. The fact that he can conceive of it does not mean it is there. Indeed the most divine aspect of man is the ability to conceive of the absolute. The grasp is greater than the reach; that is the final nobility of the creature."

While I pulled grass, taking care not to disturb the tender tentative roots of stolons that had reached out beyond the rows to make new strawberry plants, I thought about choices, decisions, and new reachings-out in the human world.

A strawberry patch, in which one is kneeling and close to the earth, is a good place for thinking about the ability, or lack of it, for making decisions. What determines the decisions or choices a man makes? Or what equipment he shall have for making them? No man selects his own mental or physical inheritance, any more than a grass plant can decide to be a strawberry stolon and therefore welcome in the strawberry patch, or remain grass, welcome on pastures and yards and on old graves.

Man's components are selected by some chance or authority beyond his control. He does not even select the environment into which this genetic combination is thrust at his birth. In his later years he may be able to choose the environment, but by that time the early unselected environment has left its indelible imprint on him, and therefore has shaped his choices and decisions.

All over the farm I find admirable instances of plants calling on their unaccustomed genetic abilities to meet emergencies. A peach seed, sprouting uninvited in the crack between a stone step and a housewall, leans forward, snatches what sun and food it can, and eventually produces bloom and fruit. Weeds mowed in the pasture, late in summer, call on their emergency growing ability and are able to produce and ripen seeds in the greatly shortened time thus allotted to them.

In the combinations of genes contained in man's heredity there is probably so great a range of potential that in his whole lifetime no man could discover, much less use, more than a small part. Undoubtedly man has in his genetic potential the ability to survive more emergencies than this earth has thus far subjected him to. He is shaped by earth at the same time he is shaping it. There is an order and consistency in this interaction which suggest the existence of an attainable, though now unprovable, absolute.

Between the mountains of heredity and environment lies a narrow valley in which each person may exercise his individual talent. This talent is faithfulness, a special kind of courage, third in the great triumvirate of existence, and through it, each person moves toward his individual destiny.

Unquestionably he still has a long way to go. Mankind is, as Hosea in anguish and yearning said long ago of his son Ephraim, "a cake not turned."

And no one can say how much longer he will have to hover before the fire.

For man is a newcomer on earth, and still so young it is impossible to say what he will be when he becomes a turned cake. There is no assurance yet that he is even as much as half-baked. It seems likely he will be more capable, more free, more loving, and vastly more intelligent rather than less.

The subconscious mind that comes out and frolics outrageously when the conscious mind is asleep, and never becomes dormant as the conscious mind does, that also brings up long-stored memories of unexpected times, or gives valid ideas called "inspirations," cannot be dominated completely by the trained, conscious mind. The subconscious sometimes plays jokes on the sleeper by dreams full of detail but quickly snatched out of the conscious memory when one tries later to tell them or write them down.

This uncontrolled intelligence gives a hint of the future mind. The present conscious mind, in comparison with the future, is like a mole's heaped-up mound compared with the whole west pasture.

SCIENTISTS TELL US birds developed wings from what in their prehistoric ancestors was a pair of front feet, but man developed his marvelous exploding brain into a faculty of imagination to serve him as wings. To adapt he does not adjust his body form, but instead exerts his brain to create a tool by which to accomplish what he wishes.

Deep down in his subconscious mind, where his future and greatest intelligence still lies undeveloped and his computerlike memory holds everything that has happened to him, man probably still has the memory of a time before he made the choice between hands and wings, and might as easily have chosen wings. This is perhaps the basis of man's eternal dream of personal flight.

It is thrilling to watch a hawk sail gracefully above a lofty forest, or even a buzzard above a farm cornfield. To watch any bird in flight is a vicarious satisfaction of man's deep-rooted dream. To this extent any bird, even the unwelcome starling, pays for the hospitality it takes at the farm feeder.

I have fed our farm-hatched mallards from my hand, and carried them in an apron pocket to warm and shelter them when they were little and solitary, and have handled them as adults, too, and now when I see them rise up from the barnlot or pasture and fly, I think, thrilled, "I can do that, too. All I need is to believe it, and I could do it, too."

🐦 BRINK STILLWATER, farmer, said, "What I like about winter is, it's gittin' on toward spring."

"Om Mane Padme Houm"

❧ WHEN I WENT DOWN to Montie's one day in late summer a large green-and-black Argiope spider was sitting in a web she had made against the screen door, which is not opened as often as a door would be in a lived-in house. It had seemed to the orb weaver like a place where food and privacy would be available.

The Argiope makes a final flamboyant line of heavy

white zigzag stitching in the center of her finished web as if it had been torn and repaired. Nearsightedly then she sits waiting for the web to vibrate, which means some food prospect has walked onto a delicate thread and the Argiope then rushes down and paralyzes it with a quick sting.

The vibration is a genuine communication to the spider; she knew the difference when I tossed small bits of grass onto the web, and she ignored them.

When I went back later in the fall, she had added the jug-shaped brown paper sack in which she would leave hundreds of eggs, unattended to but provided for, to carry on her species. She would not survive the winter.

In spring a few young spiderlings would emerge, healthy, well fed, having eaten their weaker siblings. This is Argiope's way of providing food for her young; and nature's way of making sure the species will survive without overpopulation. It seems an admirable system in the Argiope world, but applied to the human world, where overpopulation is a constant threat, it wakens an uneasy thought: Must man, for survival, be his own predator?

Mud wasps have a different way of leaving food for the young that will hatch after the wasps are gone. Organ-pipe mud wasps build nests against the unpainted inside walls of the garage here all summer. The nests vary in number of cells, and the cells vary in color, depending on the source of mud. For most of them, probably, the mud is brought from the big pond in the west pasture, which is always damp around its red-brown rim. The wasp gathers up a little ball of mud which she brings to the nest and rolls out flat, laying it diagonally from the side to the center of the cell. Each long cell, therefore, has a ribbed texture, a cut-on-the-bias look. The new cell is built against the previous one and the finished mud nest looks like the mythical pipes of Pan and suggests music.

Having made one cell long enough, the wasp then catches a spider, stings it into immobility without killing it, and puts it into the cell, lays an egg over it, and seals the cell, before going on to construct the next one.

The hatchling, finding the spider alive but in a coma, will eat it before emerging. Not all eggs will hatch, however; nature provides the mud wasp with predators that break into the cell to eat the larva. Not in malice or for sport, but from hunger.

Where the going is rough, nature increases the numbers. As man has learned by using chemicals to control insects, nature enables insects to develop bodily resistance to chemicals. Nature controls insects with other insects and other creatures.

A large green tomato worm that almost exactly matches the color of leaves and green tomatoes in my garden, nibbles them, then betrays its presence by the black pellets of its droppings. This is the larva of the hawk- or sphinx moth, and its predator is the braconid wasp that lays its eggs in the worm. When the wasplings hatch, their food is at hand. By the time they have made their small, white, oval cocoons attached to the outside of the tomato worm, it is already limpening and done for.

If the tomato worm has been fortunate enough to escape me and its insect predators, it will presently spin itself a partial cocoon that has a handlelike loop at the front end to accommodate a later-developing long tongue with which to suck nectar out of flowers. It pupates in this cocoon, usually in the ground. I have found these and taken them into the house, to watch their progress. To see the hawkmoth emerge, after weeks of having heard it rustle and tap inside the cocoon, to watch the wings unfold, imperceptibly but magically lengthening, and harden, inspires a sense of wonder that is akin to a state of prayer.

An unsprayed apple tree offers another and different example of food-and-cradle combination in the insect world. The codlin moth, detested by orchardists, lays its eggs on the lovely apple blossoms in spring. The petals fall as the green apple develops, and the moth's egg develops at the apple's core. An orchardist is greatly annoyed to bite into an apple and find it already occupied, but from the standpoint of the apple tree, the codlin moth has done a service. To the tree, the apple is important only for its seed, and if too many seeds live and grow, the parent tree will have too much competition for the available food and space. Under normal circumstances an apple tree lives many years. It is only for the pleasure and convenience of humans that it is important for the tree every year to bear great numbers of wormless apples.

☙ SUNDAY AFTERNOON when several people were in the process of leaving or arriving, Dick picked up a dragonfly from the stoned parking area and handed it to me. The left forewing had been partially pulled away from the long, narrow body. The wingspan was nearly three inches. The dragonfly fluttered, but could not lift its body.

I brought it to the back porch and laid it on my desk to study when everyone would be gone.

Unlike beetles, dragonflies cannot fold their wings over their backs, or touch them together like the covers of a book as some butterflies do when resting. Both pairs of dragonfly wings are held straight out from the side, like the wings of early airplanes. Yet even with this primitive wing arrangement the order Odonata is a marvel of speed and accuracy. The dragonfly has been known to reach a speed of forty to sixty miles an hour for short distances.

Why the injured insect was so far from water was a mystery. Like birds, they have their individual areas of authority in which they are excellent predators, and usually stay there. Possibly it had escaped from a bird that managed to carry it as far as the driveway. A dragonfly is not easy to capture.

It hatches from a nymph that has lived in fresh water. The nymph splits down the center and the young fly emerges, ready to make its way in the world. Because it catches small insects and is in turn eaten by larger creatures, the dragonfly is an important link in the balance of life at the pond.

The wings, nearest to where they set onto the body, were marked off into patches of shiny, dark brown, the color of sugar melted and burned in the skillet for making a burnt-sugar cake. The outer parts were transparent, thin as blue smoke. Lines of glinting bronzy-brown marked them off into irregular sections like pieces in a stained-glass window.

These lines are the veins that carry life and air to the wings. Other long, dark lines marked off the long body and prothorax into sharp-cornered rectangles of dusty blue, the color of ripe plums.

All insects have less vision than people have. The dragonfly's huge compound eyes nearly cover his head and each one has as many as a thousand facets, each giving just one glimpse. The insect can detect motion quickly and has to, for motion means either food or danger. Midges, gnats, and mosquitoes, caught in flight, are his customary food.

The dragonfly's distinctive weapon is its thickened underlip, which, being flexible at the base, can be thrust forward a third of the length of the body when food catching makes it necessary. The long, thorny legs, placed well forward under the body, serve also somewhat as baskets for carrying food.

Naturalists believe that the dragonfly's ancestor, Meganeura, that lived about 200 million years ago in the Carboniferous era, had a wingspan of thirty inches. There is also some organic evidence that these insects were originally terrestrial and later moved to water because food catching was easier there.

When I came back into the house half an hour later, the dragonfly had composed its body into a posture of dignity, and was dead.

🕊 NOW THE UNGATHERED SOYBEAN fields bristle with pigweed. The orchestration of crickets, katydids, jarflies, harvestflies, and associates goes on all day and all night, too. By moonrise it is going at brisk tempo. By half past two in the morning it has subsided to a slow, swinging chorus, agreeable to listen to.

A listener can pick out individual voices and examine them, and afterwhile let them go back into one subdued, sleep-inducing fugue.

One voice, a long, steadily repeated note, seems always to come from far out in the east pasture, singing of old, remembered places and times. Another, nearer the house, mumbles like a person in sleep. One makes the sustained clicking sound of a mechanical toy being wound up, and another drums in two syllables as if pressed for time, and there are always the little cadenza voices that seem to have arrived late and on the run. Some voices sing harshly. One in particular is the short, hard tone of a violin when the bow is lifted and brought down hard, briefly, on a string.

Every night from late August until frost numbs the little fiddlers the performance will be repeated, except on nights of rain, and although the country air actually throbs with soft noise, the night is called quiet.

As the cold increases, the tempo slows; some performers drop out. In the thinning background, the remaining voices sound more musical and brave.

This orchestration is a trademark of late-summer autumn, and considering the close integration between elements of the natural world, it seems likely that it is a time mark by which the unsinging ones know it is time to prepare for winter.

Possibly the wasps, bumblebees, hornets, and spiders that do not live through winter hear the autumn song as a signal to prepare for death. In general, insects and creatures of the natural world give themselves to death in an admirable kind of dignity. Possibly, to them death seems as routine as any other part of life, as expectable as food getting or egg production.

In the natural world death is not an enemy, but a part of life, the opposite only of birth. Probably it is true also in the world of humankind, and life there might be more significant if death could be accepted as an essential part of it, rather than an unnatural enemy to be fought off and evaded as long as possible, even until all shreds of dignity and purpose are gone.

🗸 IN THE LOBBY of the Union Building, where the Fine Arts Department regularly exhibits art objects and the exhibits differ from time to time, the object that evening was a Tibetan prayer apron. It looked like an openwork screen, eighteen inches square, of which bars were lengths of bone, and were interspersed with pea-sized ivory beads. Each row terminated in one, two, or three small brass bells. The bones were delicately carved in little designs of flowers, animals, and people.

"Made of Human Bones," said the card beside the prayer apron.

It was a sobering thought to carry with us as we walked on upstairs to the auditorium to see an Audubon film.

"But I don't know," said Anita Frazier, a realistic and loving woman, and well read. "It might be nice to have your bones immortalized like that, in beauty."

I made a mental note to ask the Fine Arts Department more about the bone apron.

"Harris and I think cremation is the most civilized way of disposal," continued Anita. When she speaks so earnestly, she speaks so distinctly you can hear italics in her sentences. "There are laws about it, though. Do you know you can't just have your ashes scattered around wherever you like, but must have them put into a suitable container?"

This is not a requirement in Tibet, where the bone apron is used in meditation and prayer. The Tibetans,

Buddhists, do not believe in interment in the ground. They believe nothing should be wasted. Tibetans have a choice of three ways of disposing of the body after life has completely left it, the spirit going, as they believe, to whatever reward it has earned on this earth.

The body can be thrown into the mountains, where the air is intensely cold and dry, there to become food for birds and wild beasts and eventually material for bone aprons; or burned; or thrown into a river to become food for fish. This I learned the next day from Professor Thubton Norbu, a Tibetan who has been in the United States for fourteen years. For the past three years he has taught the Uralic, Altaic, and Tibetan languages, and Tibetan civilization, at Indiana University. An anthropologist, educated in Tibet, he is the older brother of the exiled Dalai Lama, religious and political leader of Tibet.

Professor Norbu has a wife and three pre-kindergarten children and speaks excellent English, carefully. He is a Buddhist. He believes Tibet's practical philosophy of body disposal derives more from Tibet's East Indian than from its Chinese heritage.

This sparsely populated country, formed originally, scientists think, by a collision of continents that pushed up a mass of ocean bed with trimmings from the East Indian and Asian coasts, has an elevation of 14,000 feet above sea level. Grass grows in its valleys. Some fruit, nuts, and grain, especially barley, are produced. Bone carving is a trade learned by observing and doing.

Professor Norbu loves his native country. "All Tibetans wish to return to their native country," he said sadly, "if we can ever regain freedom there."

Seeing the bone apron had given me a lasting interest in Tibet and I continued my research about it.

Later in the summer my sister Miriam, writer of children's books, was visiting the farm and we were walking down to the woods back of Ira's barn. She has traveled a great deal and read vastly, and has an astonishing range and depth of information.

Some distance back of Ira's barn is the stump of a big white oak Ira and Bent cut years ago, to make clapboards for roofing the barn and silo. It took them all day to cut that giant. Later they tried to burn the stump but the wood was hard, the stump burned slowly and never burned completely. It made a convenient place to lay sticks and pieces of stone and broken fence wire that hamper the mowing or cattle grazing, and there is quite a collection around it now.

As we passed it Miriam exclaimed, "What's this? A Tibetan prayer heap?"

She said, "In Tibet they pile up stones this way. Every time they go past they lay on another stone and make a prayer." She looked around for another stick. Finding none handy, she picked up a timber-sized thistle stalk and laid it on the heap.

"What is the prayer?" I asked, adding a piece of beautifully weathered limestone, full of ancient fossils, and making my own private prayer.

"'Om mane padme houm,'" she said. "It means something like 'Oh, lotus jewel.' The lotus, you know, has great significance to the people of Tibet."

We walked on toward the fence, from where we could look down between hills and see the little creek running cleanly over its stone bed.

"Do you know," I asked, "in Tibet they do not bury their dead, but take them up into the mountains and leave them?"

"Yes, I know," Miriam answered, "and I think their way is much more loving and civilized than our dreadful funerals and burials."

"Erma doesn't think so," I told her. "She was very angry because her brother's wife had his body cremated. She said, 'You know, it's absolutely unchristian; the Bible forbids it.' "

"People accept the idea slowly," Miriam said, "but I don't believe the Bible forbids it. And you know there are still a great many people, intelligent, kind, loving people, who still fiercely reject the theory of evolution. You have to let them think what they want to. You can't live other people's lives for them."

❧ IN OCTOBER the extrasensory wisdom of woolly caterpillars sends them out to hunt winter shelter. Furry caterpillars in their black, brown, or buff coats, or combinations of these colors, appear on the porch and around the housewall, moving numbly as if they had already stayed out one frost too long.

They carry a certain amount of prestige, even in this day of scientific weather predicting. Farmers say the caterpillar's color foretells the winter weather; the darker the caterpillar's coat, the more severe the winter.

If you touch this furred larva it will curl up quickly into a little ball, like a pair of socks rolled up and tossed inaccurately at the laundry basket.

Nobody knows whether the caterpillar just takes the first suitable niche he finds or keeps hunting until his strength gives out, but when he finds the place he gives himself up to sleep. Waking in spring, he spins some silk, tears out his own hair, and weaves himself a brown cocoon the texture of old-time felt boots. Inside of it, he continues his life adventure toward its next phase, which is to become an Isabella moth, a small yellow-orange, winged creature with dark spots scattered haphazardly over its wings. Pretty, but never spectacular. In the natural world, however, categories are not divided into pretty or ugly, or good or bad, but merely does or does not adapt and consequently does or does not survive.

HUMAN SYMPATHY goes out to whichever creature is the leading character in the story. In a hawk story, for example, the reader would not grieve overmuch to know the hawk had taken seventeen young Bantams and eight young guineas on the farm this summer. But in a book about farm poultry, this is tragedy and the guineas know it.

Fortunately for the rest of her creatures, nature has provided that there will be fewer hawks than field mice or guineas. It is a thrifty world, admirable if one can look at it impersonally. Being impersonal is not a human characteristic. Man wants the world his way, the way he thinks is most comfortable, convenient, or beautiful. He is relentlessly determined to say which creatures are good, and which bad, and therefore which shall live and which shall be wiped out.

Even while he is protecting his poultry, a farmer has to wonder how far he has a right to interfere; how far, in fact, for his own welfare, he may interfere.

MY SISTER MIRIAM once lived in a small town where there were a great many Catholics and factory workers, which was fortunate for her because she was never a handy person with saw and hammer, although she was unsurpassed with typewriter and words, especially for children.

Once when a workman was repairing her screen door he stopped suddenly because he had discovered an insect on the door's screen. A large one, somewhat resembling a grasshopper, except it had the ability to look back over its shoulder at him, something no ordinary insect can do. Miriam suggested carrying it safely outside.

The man was shocked and exclaimed sincerely, "Oh, no, I couldn't disturb him now. It's a praying mantis and he's praying."

A devout Lutheran, Miriam was also a naturalist and most of her books were about animals, so the praying mantis was allowed to finish his devotions undisturbed. Perhaps the workman silently joined him. Certainly a little time spent in prayer could not have done the carpenter any harm, especially if he was being paid by the hour.

Actually what the praying mantis is trying to do in his praying posture is to look sinister and thereby frighten away his enemies. It is a common defense in the insect world and sometimes it works. Sometimes it works in the human world, too, where prayer is more a state of mind than a physical or intellectual posture. In the human world it is an outgrowth of personal experience and thinking, with some suffering thrown in, and although science has not yet discovered its genetic construction, prayer is in no way in conflict with science.

Being in a state of prayer, whether kneeling traditionally, or sitting cross-legged like a Buddhist, or lying down, or even on the run, is strengthening to the person who believes in its effectiveness. Sometimes, seeing the cattle standing, blissful and quiet in the new sunlight, I think, "That is what a state of prayer feels like."

Or it is like an electric cord, capable of carrying energy from a great source to an instrument able to make use of it. It is even comparable to a commonplace kitchen ingredient, baking powder, which a farmwife puts into biscuits, casually, with confidence that it will leaven them.

Public prayer, spoken aloud, is impersonal but sometimes unites people in a common feeling and gives them a sense of having met some useful requirement. I prefer silent prayer, perhaps because of my father's early Quaker habit of silent grace at meals. His children did not understand, or appreciate, this silence. It was a custom to be observed because "Papa says so" and Papa was to be obeyed unless you could make sure of not getting caught. Before bowing his head he always looked around the table at every one of us, including the cousins and hired men and, on washdays, Aunt Claire Adkins, the kindly fat neighbor who washed for us down by the Big Spring in summer. Then he closed his eyes and, as we called it in secret irreverence, "went into the silence."

My mother's Ohio-dwelling parents were devout Methodists, accustomed to morning and evening prayers spoken aloud by her father, while everybody knelt at chairs. Grandpa "asked the blessing" before meals. To adopt the Quaker silence must have been an adjustment, perhaps welcome, to my mother.

In my own prayers, which are as indispensable to me as my morning coffee, or food, or sleep, I like to be alone, where I am sure nobody will interrupt while I think my reverent thoughts and listen for whatever answer or new thought is thereby evoked, and feel the sense of Presence that sometimes arises. A prayer can be made at any time of day, or in any place, of course.

My brother and my five sisters and I were all taught the traditional "Now I lay me down to sleep," but I never really even guessed the realistic value and power of prayer until I was old enough to have known adult joy and pain, love and apprehension. For the person who believes in it, prayer is comparable to the pulleys farmers use, called "block and tackle," by which a small tractor is able to lift a mighty load. Quarry men call this "shives."

Prayer is not necessarily emotional or intellectual exercise. It is, imperatively, spiritual, and addressed to whatever authority one considers supremely valid.

Neither is it like ordering something out of a Sears sale catalogue, although when the answer comes it is direct, personal, and for the person who believes in it, an unfailing source of endurance.

꙳ THEY COME FROM EVERYWHERE, from nowhere, suddenly collected around whatever draws them: vinegar gnats around a bitten apple, people around an accident, fight, or fire.

People want to hear about misfortune, wars, deaths, disasters, the bad news. Partly because inherent in man's developing subconscious mind is the knowledge that change is inevitable and necessary, the very core of evolution.

But probably the greater reason for people's fascination with bad news is spiritual, based in the deep subconscious mind where in pity and gratitude the onlooker thinks, "There but for the grace . . ." This is, in its way, a prayer of thanksgiving.

People who say, "I never pray," are therefore as inaccurate as people who say, "I never dream." For everybody prays, either consciously or unconsciously. Prayer is any thought or emotion that acknowledges a relationship between mankind and his fellow citizens of earth, and their mutual creative authority.

↯ "No," said BRINK STILLWATER kindly, "I wouldn't call Iry bald, but when he mentions his hair, you know which one he means."

"The Violets Have Got to Go"

🐦 SURELY IF there is a commonplace thing in the world, a toad is it. But the one I found sitting in a place scooped out of the wet, cold ground near the hen's house today was bright brown, splotched, and genuinely attractive. I brought it into the house for a personal interview.

It seemed uncommunicative, but on the porch, surrounded by books, it answered some of my questions, and created several more.

It belonged to an ordinary Midwest family, Bufonidae, an "amphibian anurous batrachian," which means it is tailless and can live on land or in water. Adult toads live on land, but return to the water in March or April to lay their eggs in long, viscid strings. The eggs, fertilized as they are ejected, hatch in two or three days. Within six weeks, especially in floodtime, the resultant tadpoles have developed into toads and leave the water in such numbers that people say "it rained toads."

Sitting squattily on its hind legs in a glass jar on my desk, the batrachian supported itself on the bent front legs. The toes spread apart as if reaching for a long chord on the piano. The warty body reminded me of a garden squash from which mud has been wiped off hastily and not well.

The head is made of three triangles, meeting at their sharpest points, all set onto a flat base which is the toad's chin. The pale underthroat and a spot back of the shoulders pulsated while the toad and I regarded each other. There is a line down the center of his back, as in a cloth toy made in two pieces and stitched together. Warts, which are bony deposits in the glands, are arranged in an attractive pattern of dots and dashes on the back. Behind the eyes are two large masses from which the toad can eject an irritating liquid into the eyes or wounds of his enemies.

Shakespeare to the contrary, this toad is neither venomous nor really ugly. For defense it depends chiefly on protective coloration or playing dead. If it has time it can breathe in enough air to inflate its body beyond a snake's swallowing power. Naturalists insist that the quick spurt of urine . . . a toad's way of saying "no comment" . . . does not cause warts.

The "precious jewel" in the toad's head is his swift, pointed tongue, which is fastened to the front rather than at the back of his mouth and is therefore able to flick out and catch an insect faster than the human eye can follow or the unlucky insect depart.

After the interview I returned Bufonida to the scoop-out and as soon as possible it left for a place less accessible to interviewers.

The startling thought occurred to me that man also is anurous and to some extent amphibian. For the most part he lives on land, but increasingly returns to water for recreation. As his numbers increase and his technical and financial abilities enable, he creates watering places to play in. Too often, thus re-forming earth nearer to his heart's desire, he seriously damages it.

His playgrounds become clotted with possessions and debris. Unlike ancient people who could move on when their midden heaps outgrew them, man cannot escape; he has less space to move into. In his playgrounds he appears in such numbers an observing toad could say, "It rained people; they are ugly and venomous and yet wear a precious jewel in their heads."

In man's head the precious jewel is his imagination.

Some conservationists fear man's damage to earth has gone beyond his ability to repair or control it. Some believe the menace is a chain reaction, inescapable because of requirements of modern living. Others believe that having unwittingly created the problem, man has the imagination necessary to control it.

Still another group comforts itself with the scientific prediction that in another few billion years our sun will burn out or explode as other stars have done, and so what difference does it make? These people are neither cynical nor indifferent to modern problems.

And the rest of us who speak earnestly to earth and also listen and think we sense in it an over-all design, even though incomprehensible to us, what shall we believe? That the design has a logical beginning and an inevitable outcome? Assuming a design, what is man's assigned role in it?

Man's passion to understand himself is as ancient and compulsive as his instincts for reproduction and self-preservation. The creative spark in humankind that impels him to pray, or think, or sing, or build a house, is the same spark that makes him restless, curious, destructive. Unquestionably it is the same spark that has driven him since his infancy to seek answers to the eternal questions: Who am I, and from where did I come, and what am I here for?

↯ IN BEAUTIFUL bell-like prose John Donne said, "No man is an island unto himself entire . . ."

But in truth every man, at some time in his life, is an island unto himself, ringed by a bleak shore. Before him lies a vast fullness identical with a vast emptiness, and no one can come to him there, neither friend to comfort nor enemy to torment.

There, in loneliness and pain, he discovers the boundaries of his soul. And if the boundaries are thereby enlarged, even if ever so little, mankind is thereby drawn a step nearer to its ultimate emergence.

"The Violets Have Got to Go"

Now AND THEN a starling finds its way down the chimney and comes out into the kitchen at Montie's house and of course it is never able to find its way out again. Confused and terrified, it cannot see the door I have propped open until I drive it to the opening. When at last it feels the open air and sees the familiar sky, it goes out with a cry of joy. The ecstasy of freedom regained is in that cry and makes me, for a moment, a kinsman of the starling. For to humankind freedom is sometimes more precious than life itself.

Once, walking in the desert back yard of my sister Nina's house in Arizona, I came suddenly upon a bird dangling in air just ahead of me on the path. It had become entangled in a nylon kite string caught in an oleander bush and stretching across the path into a palo verde tree.

It was a young gambel quail. I have never been so close to one before and in my excited pity I was able to break the strong nylon string with bare hands, being careful not to injure the bird further. In the bird's efforts to extricate itself, it had got the string so wrapped around one wing and leg that I would have to have had scissors to remove the cord. I carried it quickly into the house and Nina cut the bindings with nail scissors while I held the resigned and trembling bird. I also trembled and Nina trembled. Then, assuming it would want a drink immediately, we carried it outside to a shallow pool in the yard. We were so eager to help it we scarcely took time to examine it, but set it beside the pool. Aware that it was once again free, the quail turned and ran quickly under the fence and out into the desert. Its joy was as apparent as the little footprints it left beside the pool.

AUDREY WILSON WAS STANDING in her front yard, looking at a clump of pale-yellow jonquils, as I came home. I stopped, and Audrey came down to the car, bending over to look and talk. "Bending is good for my back," she said, declining to get in. Her back trouble is the result of an automobile accident a few years ago in which she was badly injured and her mother-in-law, riding with her, was killed.

"I think Grandma Fannie must have planted these Easter flowers," she said. "I can't remember them being here when Mom and Dad lived here and we were children."

We talked about Audrey's father, John, a large, boisterous man who loved a hearty joke and would go to any effort to make one. In an ice-cream-eating contest once, John got as far as a start on the third quart. His conversation was always interesting; he was keenly observant and expressed himself freely in good, made-up words such as "caviness" for canvas, "savich" for sandwich, "donged" for dawned. When he said, "It finally donged on me," he meant, "I finally realized."

He was inventive, a good mechanic and carpenter, but less good as a farmer. Sometimes on the farm he grew restless and went off for a day, telling nobody where he was going or when he would be back. As a child, Audrey went with him whenever she could. "I just loved to hear the stories and the conversations with people," she said. "I wish I'd written it all down."

When he had some carpentering project that puzzled him John never worried. "I just went to bed and slep' on it," he told me, "and the next morning I had the answers." He had "hunches." Audrey says she inherits this. Her hunches deal mostly with family affairs.

"The Violets Have Got to Go"

"The year before Dad died," she said, "I often woke in the night with a deep feeling of oppression. I used to get up and walk it off." The spring breeze ruffled the pale-yellow jonquils at Audrey's feet as she talked.

"The night before Dad died I got up and walked and reasoned with myself but that night I couldn't shake it off. Mom told me later Dad had done the same thing that night."

This sensitivity, often called ESP, is probably a developing sense in humankind, rather than a vestigial ability. In the future edition of humankind the hunch and the prophetic dream may be a part of the common equipment, as much as our present five senses are to us.

Audrey said, "After Dad's death I told Mom, 'There's more to come. There's something else we have to be prepared for.' I had a hunch."

Two weeks later when the newly planted corn was barely visible in green lines across the field, Audrey was driving a car that was struck by another car veering out of the road. The surgeon who repaired her face had to work from a photograph. By the time she was able to leave the hospital, farmers were in the cornfields, picking the ripe corn.

Audrey is not bitter, or self-pitying, or a recluse. She laughs a quick, honest laugh, does the housework with Johnny's help, visits neighbors, and helps in the garden from which they always have a surplus to give the neighbors.

Audrey Wilson is a paragraph about human courage, readable and lighthearted as a spring jonquil.

⅄ Nora Carter was a person of courage. I saw her only once and always intended to go back and visit her again, but I never did.

I met her when I went with Dick to look at a "family" milk cow Jim Carter had offered to sell.

Every now and then, in this era of convenience and specialization when most farmers buy safe, homogenized milk and cultured buttermilk and thin cream called "half and half" in convenient paper cartons, Dick gets a yearning for a milk cow. "For the sake of all that good cream to take to Brotherhood suppers," he says, but actually it's because a farmer believes every farm ought to be self-supplying in the way of food.

The sample of Guernsey milk Jim Carter sent home with us that evening was cream to a fourth of its depth next morning.

The Carters were in their living room and Jim got up to go with Dick to look at the cow. "You just as well stay here with me," said Nora Carter from her cane-seated chair beside the tall floor lamp. Under the ruffle of her cap, the bright brown eyes told me, "Please stay with me. I am lonely." I stayed.

"You know I had a stroke about four years ago," she said as I sat down on a chair opposite her. She has also arthritis, diabetes, a heart ailment, and some other discomforts, but she doesn't complain. Her spirit is as refreshing as rain on a hot summer day.

Jim does most of the housework, she said, in addition to his farm work and working at the Owen County sale barn and doing custom hay baling.

The living room was clean and bare of rug. We had come in through the kitchen, as farmers customarily do, and I had noticed supper dishes drying in a rack and a little piece of apple pie on the table.

Mrs. Carter sews some on the machine that stands in front of dish-filled shelves in the living room. By holding on to various pieces of furniture she can get to the kitchen stove to cook her own meals when Jim is away.

The tillable half of their two-hundred-acre farm is in pasture and hay. Mrs. Carter seldom gets outdoors. Most of the time she sits by the window, through which she can see the highway and farm fields, and the deer that come from a nearby government reserve. "Sometimes as many as fifteen or twenty," she said. "They're pretty but they ruin the farmers' soybeans."

She grew up on a small farm along the Texas Pike in Owen County and went to a one-room country school near there. When she was a child she picked wild blackberries and carried them to the county-seat town to sell for twenty cents a gallon.

As a young woman during World War II, she kept a boardinghouse in Indianapolis. She enjoyed this time. A framed photograph of her, taken in those years, was hanging on the wall behind her. It showed an attractive, happy-looking young woman with neatly curled, dark hair. She looks businesslike and is wearing a white blouse. She met Jim when he came to stay at her boardinghouse. He served in the Army and while in service made up his mind to farm.

They started with a small farm near Mooresville, then had a larger one near Quincy, then, gaining courage, bought the two-hundred-acre Owen County farm near Vandalia. Nora missed the city at first, she said, "but in those days I was strong and well and could work hard."

She has no children, no brothers or sisters, no living parent. She doesn't care to read and TV makes her nervous. She used to piece quilts and even made one for her dog. It was new and pretty and he was lying on it, on the sofa, as we talked. "He's my faithful companion," she said fondly. He lifted his ears and looked back at her.

Asked "What gives you the most pleasure?" she said promptly, "Sleep." Then she smiled. "I like to lie down in daytime because it feels so comfortable, but I don't sleep then. I sleep well at night."

She likes her neighbors. "They're good to me. Last spring two of them came and cleaned the house all over and wouldn't take any money for it."

When Dick came back and we were leaving, she stood up suddenly and took a few careful steps. Then in a touching gesture of friendliness, she took my hand and walked with us to the kitchen door.

"Now do come back," she urged, and stayed there, supporting herself by a holding to the screen door while we went out and down the steps to the car.

⅄ "AND ALL WENT to be taxed, everyone into his own city."

Every person goes into his own country to be taxed, and every person pays his tax in the coin of his own spirit.

The night Uncle Bent Stanger's wife, Evvie, died, he went out to his woodpile in the back yard and split kindling all night.

⅄ CHARLIE ANDERSON was a hundred years old on the sixth of March. He lives alone on his forty-acre farm near the Owen-Clay county line, and does his own farming and housekeeping. His sixty-five-year-old son Albert, who lives near, comes often. Every Monday and Tuesday they go to livestock sales at Morton and Cloverdale. Albert drives. Charlie, who drove a stock truck hauling hogs and cattle to the Indianapolis livestock yards until he was eighty-six years old, didn't renew his license last year when he was ninety-nine.

Charlie doesn't hear as well as when he was attending the one-room Kiser school through all eight grades; his hair is now an almost invisible fuzz on top of his head and his small mustache is mixed with gray, and he has no teeth, but he has an excellent memory, a sharp mind, an engaging twinkle in his blue-gray eyes, and he is witty. He is five feet two inches tall and never has weighed more than a hundred fifty pounds. He walks ably, whistling softly as he walks, and his health is good, "I don't doctor," he said, twinkling. One of his two grandsons is a doctor.

Charlie's house sits on a steep, high hill. When its yard needs mowing, Charlie shuts the road gate at the foot of the hill and opens the pasture gate at the other side of it and the cattle come into the yard and eat the grass and clover. Inside, his house has a swept, uncluttered look. You stand on the porch and knock at the front door, and from inside, and without knowing who it is, Charlie calls out, "Come in, come in!"

The living room is carpeted with two patterns of carpet, both worn and well swept. The bed is in one corner, neatly made. Charlie was shaven and wearing clean work clothes although he had not been expecting guests. The TV is in that room. "I don't like TV," Charlie confessed. "I get the news and the stock market and then I'm done with it."

His winter fuel-oil stove is in another corner, its pilot light burning the year round. "And I wouldn't take a nickel for it, either," said Charlie proudly, and on that hot July afternoon turned up the flame to show how easily the stove is controlled.

He gave his three guests the three rockers, then went to the kitchen and got a straight chair for himself, from near the round table where he eats his meals.

There was a buffet in the front room and on the wall above it hung a large, tinted photograph in a frame. It showed a handsome young man with dark, thick hair, twinkling eyes, and sensitive mouth, and beside him a shy, pretty young woman.

"Is that your wedding picture?" I guessed, and Charlie, pleased, nodded and smiled. He and Inez were married on December 27, 1897, he told us. They went to housekeeping "on the home place," which was her father's farm. They lived there several years. Their two daughters and Albert were born there. Ethel died at twenty-one of diphtheria, leaving a three-day-old baby. Mary died at fifteen. "Inez has been dead fifty-five years," Charlie said. A photograph of her hangs above the TV. He sits where he faces her while he gets the weather and livestock reports. "I look at her more than I do at the TV," he said.

He has lived on four other farms besides his present one and the home place "and never more than three miles from Poland," he added, twinkling. Poland is a little town in Clay County, known for Kattman's General Store and the lovely, old, restored Poland church.

In his earlier farming days Charlie traded in livestock and started the weekly livestock sale at Poland.

His kitchen had not much furniture in it. There was no clutter or unwashed dishes or food sitting around. The round table sits by a window and a couple more of the straight-backed, pretty chairs were drawn up to it. Charlie cooks sometimes on a small electric hotplate in the kitchen, but every day he cooks something on the iron cookstove he bought seventy-five years ago when he and Inez started housekeeping. Her pretty, blue-flowered cups and saucers and plates are sitting on a shelf in a poplar cupboard that originally belonged to her grandmother.

Charlie drinks coffee three times a day "but never between meals." He offered to make coffee for us. He likes all kinds of pie, except pumpkin. "Even as a boy I never cared for pumpkin," he said. He doesn't smoke. "I quit smoking when I was fifteen years old. I had smoked for a long time," he told us. He smoked cigars. His parents, who raised tobacco, didn't smoke but had no objection to Charlie's smoking. One day when he was fifteen years old he said suddenly, "I'm quitting," and laid his half-smoked cigar on the windowsill, where it stayed for four years. He has never smoked since, he said.

He gets up every morning at six o'clock. "Eight o'clock finds me in bed every night. Sometimes seven," he added.

A door by the refrigerator leads into his "plunder" room, where he has an electric washer and considerable other plunder. A door near the old cookstove leads into a bedroom where there is an old, pretty four-poster bed and a modern bathroom. A door near the poplar cupboard leads into Charlie's "parlor."

"Come into my parlor," invited Charlie, twinkling. The door stuck. "You can see how often I go into my parlor," said Charlie, pushing and twinkling. The parlor window was dimmed by a cloth curtain under a ragged old green window blind. The room was dusty, dimly

233

lighted, and completely fascinating because of things in
it. High on its tall walls were several framed photographs
of relatives and the "home place." A "family record" in
color and framed, but still blank, stood on the floor. There
were more of the dining chairs there and some bureaus.
An album bulging with old postcards embossed with
Santa Clauses, flowers, birds, children, and scenes. On a
table were dusty kerosene lamps, a stuffed bald eagle
Charlie had shot fifty years earlier not knowing what it
was. The bare floor was made of smooth, wide boards. It
was a friendly, inviting room.

"I'm so glad you came," Charlie exclaimed when we
had gone out into the yard to leave. Dick took some
pictures of him pumping the long-handled pump from
which no water came or was expected to. We promised to
come back soon, bringing a cherry pie.

WE WERE COMING HOME from someplace, in the
truck, and seeing Audrey standing in the garden amidst
tomato plants, stopped to say hello. Merely that, honestly,
with no predatory intentions.

"Can't even give 'em away," exclaimed Audrey,
laughing. "I didn't can any tomatoes at all this year. Had
enough left from last year. And I fussed at Johnny when
he set out two rows of tomato plants."

Dick offered to "help out." He wouldn't let Audrey
get a sack. "I've got an old work shirt in the truck I can
pile tomatoes on," he said, probably because it would
hold more than a sack. While we were filling it, another
neighbor came to get green tomatoes to fry.

I expressed surprise, remembering one time when
I fried them and Dick wailed, "I never was so disap-

pointed in my life. They looked like slices of wonderful meat."

"My family just loves fried green tomatoes," Mrs. Sims said. "I even can 'em."

How?

"You slice 'em pretty thick, cover 'em with salted water, and cold-pack 'em for fifteen minutes."

Then how do you cook 'em later?

"Just take 'em out of the can, dip 'em in batter, and fry 'em in a skillet. They're really good."

Do they get soft in canning?

"Not too soft," Mrs. Sims said.

🌾 IT IS JUNE and the wheat is ripening. Mornings are mild. The morning light is blue and gold, the color of contentment. The sight of a wheatfield, in its final goldenness just before the combine moves in, awakens a feeling of security, no doubt because wheat has been, since ancient times, a bulwark against hunger.

The ripening field, motionless in sunlight, seems the very symbol of peace. If the field is then gently brushed by wind the sense of peace becomes underlined by a surge of joy, a reverence in which the whole conviction of creation for a purpose is indelibly coded.

While the wheatfield ripens, roses drop their aging petals, and elderberry bushes make themselves known. You may not have noticed them earlier, but now when they are whitened with plate-sized clusters of bloom, you will notice them. And even before you see the green-white flowers you will be aware of their delicate, fruity fragrance, and the sense of June richness becomes then almost overwhelming.

235

Wild raspberries ripening earlier than the cultivated ones are large now in June and shine redly along the road despite last year's roadside spraying. A quail calls, establishing his boundary.

In this June richness the quail becomes the voice of summer. I think I could not bear any more; neither could I bear a June with less.

↓ LOOKING CLOSELY at the commonplace things of nature that are found on almost any small family farm, one becomes aware of a quality of miracle and infinity about them.

The more one researches these small things, such as the purple-blue violet I picked in the yard this morning and brought in to examine under a microscope, the more clear it becomes that nothing on earth exists totally separate and unrelated, and that every living thing is composed of ever smaller parts.

From the purple-striped deep tube of the violet's petal a naturalist could go on to an examination of the larger, related plant world, or a scientist could as easily discover the infinitely smaller parts of which the violet cells are composed. Either way, a thing as commonplace as an ordinary spring violet contains the essence of infinity.

For creation has no beginning and no end, and in our present human limitation we cannot comprehend a thing that has no beginning and no ending. We see only that as evolution continues change competes with stability. Something resists, and something initiates change . . . "the violets have got to go" . . . evolution requires destruction, reshaping, and continuing just as life requires the continuity of birth and death.

The human mind is one of the major forces of destruction, equated with fire or flood, ice, wind, and time, and the law of gravity. The determination of all living things to survive and perpetuate their kind opposes itself to nature's equally relentless determination that all must die and thereby nourish the earth and make space for new generations in which the experiment can continue.

Until now, man, believing himself the masterwork of creation, has laid no restriction on his manipulation of earth. Now earth-concern has become the insigne of this society and our philosophy of manipulation is beginning to be not so much "Can I do this?" as "Do I have a right to do this?" or "What will happen to the related earth if I do this?" We are beginning, barely, to realize that man is not the masterwork, but only a component of the masterwork, which is earth itself, and perhaps earth is only a component of a still greater masterwork.

Nevertheless, man as he now exists is a menace to earth as it now exists, and if unrestrained in his manipulations, he would probably destroy it all, including himself. Fortunately he fails in some efforts and may thereby gain time in which to mature and reach a better understanding of his real relation to earth. Fortunately also, earth is resilient, more durable than any of its components.

Religion, philosophy, and science have become a part of our developing earth-concern. We discuss the waste and conservation of our natural resources, the need of green areas, farms, breathing spaces, parks, and wilderness. Distressed by "urban sprawl" and "the decay of cities" and the alarming decrease of space for solitude which man inherently requires, we begin to understand that responsibility to earth is inseparable from man's search to know himself.

Periodically, over the billions of years of earth's existence, nature has used one or another of its destructive forces to change the shape of earth. We know that mountains have been pushed up out of oceans, or built up by violent eruption of earth's hot inner juices; that what was a polar cap ages ago is now a great desert; that earth-crust collisions have torn away land masses, changing the shapes of continents, burying some islands and creating some new ones. We have evidence that slowly melting glaciers, sliding ponderously away, have gouged out lakes and rivers, compressed sediment and sea life into stone; that immense forests have been toppled from mountains and turned to stone or swamps; that in at least one place a vast land mass was pushed up into mountain, still bearing its original river in its arms, and the river cut it into great canyons.

The pattern implies a vast, but consistent discipline. Our conception of the force changes in different times and societies, but man's persistent yearning to find his own place in creation continues to engross him through all ages and through all of his evolution. From time to time, in the search for his own identity he finds slivers of truth and must accept them, regardless of what long-cherished beliefs they may displace. In observing the commonplace things of this farm, and noting that "you cannot pluck a flower without troubling a star" (although it may be a while before the star gives evidence of having been troubled), I find an exciting kind of comfort.

Every person, as, in fact, every element of earth, has significance to earth, for however obscure or hidden away he may be, the universal laws apply to him, seek him out, and influence his behavior, just as any infinitesimal grain in a sedimentary rock, anyplace, is subject to the universal laws of gravity and magnetism.

These truths apply not only to earth's larger observable parts but equally to the ever-smaller parts of parts. Microbiologists, from their years of patient, concentrated research, show us how all parts of a living cell operate individually and precisely, what they are made of, and how they react or unite, how each one can be further divided into smaller components, and how everything works in an exquisite pattern of order and discipline, consistently.

Scientists who attribute the evolution of the living cell to "blind chance" also sometimes say of other facts, "We do not yet know" or "We may never know." A person learning of the behavior of the minute parts of a living cell is not willing to attribute this marvelous consistency and order to "blind chance." It seems plausible to believe it is produced by some basic law, truth, or disciplinary force that as yet our most brilliant scientists have not even sensed. A force we may, perhaps, never know. Or, perhaps, the knowing of which is the ultimate goal of humankind.

Perhaps in the vastly distant future it will become apparent that present man's assignment was destruction. Since it was somewhat restricted by nature's greater capability, it could be called controlled destruction, and it has served in the creation of a new earth shape and perhaps the evolution of a further emergent creature . . . the cake turned . . . greatly superior to present man.

For me, this is a comforting, strengthening thought and thoroughly valid.

Therefore, although I see that human life is inevitably marked by sadness and beauty, and humankind is sometimes noble and often exactly the opposite, and love, man's most cherished gift, is always at least half pain, the total song is neither fearful nor sad. And I would say with Christina Rossetti, "Sing no sad songs."

🕊 SAID BRINK STILLWATER, farmer, "If there is a heaven there must be a special place in it for the ordinary people who have had the courage to remain ordinary, in the face of extraordinary hardships they were called on to endure here on earth."

A Note About the Author

Rachel Peden was born in Redkey, Indiana, and was graduated from Indiana University with a degree in sociology. Since 1946 she has been writing a farm column for the Indianapolis *Star* and the Muncie *Evening Press*. Mrs. Peden and her farmer husband have two grown children and make their home near Bloomington, Indiana. Her previous books were *Rural Free* and *The Land, The People*.

A Note on the Type

This book was set in Monticello, a Linotype revival of the original Roman No. 1 cut by Archibald Binny and cast in 1796 by the Philadelphia type foundry Binny & Ronaldson. The face was named Monticello in honor of its use in the monumental fifty-volume *Papers of Thomas Jefferson*, published by Princeton University Press. Monticello is a transitional type design, embodying certain features of Bulmer and Baskerville, but it is a distinguished face in its own right.

This book was composed, printed, and bound by American Book–Stratford Press, Inc., Saddlebrook, New Jersey. Typography and binding design by Camilla Filancia.